Pearl Harbor Recalled

Pearl Harbor Recalled

New Images of the Day of Infamy

Paintings by Tom Freeman

Text by James P. Delgado

Naval Institute Press

Annapolis, Maryland

Paintings copyright © 1991 by Tom Freeman
Text copyright © 1991 by the United States Naval Institute
Annapolis, Maryland.

Library of Congress Cataloging-in-Publication Data

Freeman, Tom (Tom W.)
    Pearl Harbor recalled : new images of the day of infamy /
paintings by Tom Freeman ; text by James P. Delgado.
        p.   cm.
    Includes bibliographical references and index.
    ISBN 1-55750-251-X (alk. paper)
    1. Pearl Harbor (Hawaii), Attack on, 1941—Pictorial works.
2. Freeman, Tom (Tom W.)   I. Delgado, James P.   II. Title.
D767.92.F74   1991
940.54'26—dc20   91-29585
Printed in the United States of America on acid-free paper ∞
9 8 7 6 5 4 3 2
First printing

Frontispiece: "Daybreak of Destiny": *Arizona* and *Vestal* moored
near Ford Island just before the Japanese attack.

*To God, my country, my family, and the men and women who
gave their lives that Sunday morning.*

TOM FREEMAN

*To my father-in-law, Chuck Bremmer, and his shipmates on
USS Higbee (DD-806), who brought the war to an end with
TF 38 off Japan in July–August 1945.*

JAMES P. DELGADO

Contents

Acknowledgments

Doing a book like this requires the help of many people and organizations. The artist wishes to thank James P. Delgado, former maritime historian of the National Park Service and presently executive director of the Vancouver Maritime Museum. Jim was the one who planted the seed for this book, and he was kind enough to write the accompanying text. He also enabled me to produce an accurate account of what occurred at Pearl Harbor by putting me in touch with many of the people who knew the information.

Jeff Little, who knew I needed information on the Japanese aircraft involved in the attack, introduced me to Wesley Stachnick. Since that first meeting, Wes and I have become good friends, and his library eventually ended up in my studio. An aircraft modeler, Wes is truly an artist in his field.

My longtime friend James Diggs gave me the information on Pearl Harbor that he has collected over the years. He is as close to me as a brother, and he and his wife, Cindy, even allowed me to use their honeymoon photographs so that I could get a feel for the Hawaiian countryside.

Robert Mikish of the National Air and Space Museum put me in touch with David Aiken, who gave freely of his time and efforts, going through his vast files of data about the Japanese attack. I hope that I've done justice to the information he has given me.

Jeffrey Little neglected his hobby shop to share what he knows with me. He was able to find the models that seemed to elude everyone else. I made many calls to Jeff at the eleventh hour, and he always came through.

A friend for many years and the curator of model ships for the U.S. Naval Academy Museum, Robert Sumrall provided invaluable help with my work on the battleships.

Robert Chenowyth, the curator of the *Arizona* Memorial Museum, and Daniel Martinez, the museum's park historian, gave me abundant information about Pearl Harbor and about the attack. I'm sure that we made the telephone company very happy.

Many thanks to Jaci Day and Dee Matney of the U.S. Naval Institute.

Kenneth Hagan, James Cheevers, Ronald Corder, and Ronald Engelmeyer of the U.S. Naval Academy Museum spent much time and energy to put on an exceptional exhibit of the paintings in this collection.

My oldest and dearest friend, Donald A. Phelps, Sr., literally became my delivery service and on many occasions my chauffeur. My thanks go also to Cheryl, Don's wife, for putting up with both of us.

Travis Freeman, my oldest son, has been a fantastic model and a good sport, having to endure being photographed in an endless variety of poses.

Shane Freeman, my third child and second son, spent a lot of time building models that I did not have the time to do.

I would like to thank my sister Renee and Charles C. Sander, her husband, for without them I could not have completed this project.

I also need to thank David D'Amelio, who is not only my accountant and adviser but also my friend, for his support of this project.

Accomplishing this work would not have been at all enjoyable if my wife, Ann, and our children had not put up with this crazed person they saw morning, noon, and night. To them, I hope it was worth it.

The author wishes to acknowledge the support and research information provided by the United States Naval Institute, the Naval Historical Center, the Military History Branch of the National Archives, the Submerged Cultural Resources Unit of the National Park Service,

and the USS *Arizona* Memorial. I also thank Bob Brown
and Joe McManus, former crew members of the yard tug
Hoga, for sharing their memories of 7 December 1941.
The excellent collection of oral histories and participant
accounts at the Naval Institute were a tremendous help,
many of which were edited by Paul Stillwell and published as *Air Raid: Pearl Harbor!* by the Naval Institute
Press. I also wish to acknowledge the assistance of Paul
Ditzel, Robert Mikesh, Robert Sumrall, Daniel A. Martinez, David Aiken, Daniel J. Lenihan, and Larry Murphy. The painting of the sunken *Arizona* is based in part
on original drawings of the wreck by Jerry L. Livingston
and Larry V. Nordby of the National Park Service and
on Robert Sumrall's model of the wreck. The manuscript
was reviewed by Jesse L. Pond and Paul Stillwell and
edited by Anthony F. Chiffolo.

Introduction

Imperial Japan's nationalistic and militaristic fervor, coupled with a strong belief in Japan's divine right to rule all of Southeast Asia, brought Japan and the United States into increasing diplomatic confrontation throughout the 1930s. Compounding the problem was Japan's bloody, undeclared war to dominate China, and Britain's, France's, and Holland's weakening control of their Asian colonies as a result of the war in Europe. American diplomatic pressures and economic sanctions pushed militaristic factions in Japan closer to war. The United States was then a powerful but uncommitted force, officially neutral in the spreading global war but nonetheless ideologically and politically committed to opposing the Axis Powers.

Japan's signature of the Tripartite Pact with Germany and Italy in September 1940 further aggravated tensions with the United States. When Japan then moved to seize France's valuable colonies in Southeast Asia, as part of an agreement with the Vichy government, President

Franklin D. Roosevelt acted to block Japanese expansion in the Pacific. An American economic embargo cut off shipments of scrap steel, oil, high-octane gasoline, and other industrial commodities to Japan, while an executive order froze Japanese assets in the United States.

Facing economic ruin, and feeling that its options were severely limited, the Japanese government of Premier Hideki Tojo decided on war. The Imperial Japanese Navy feared the naval power of the U.S. Pacific Fleet, which had moved from the West Coast to Pearl Harbor, Hawaii, in 1940, and the military strength of the American bases in Guam, the Philippines, and Midway, Johnston, and Wake islands. As a result, the Imperial Japanese Navy, under the leadership of Admiral Isoroku Yamamoto, Commander-in-Chief of the Combined Fleet, made America the first priority for a Japanese attack. Yamamoto visualized an assault like the Japanese victory at Port Arthur against the more powerful Russian Navy in 1904. A bold, "strategical surprise" attack on the United States' Pacific Fleet as it lay at anchor at Pearl Harbor, Yamamoto hoped, would devastate American naval power, demoralize the American public, and secure victory in the Pacific.

At the same time, Yamamoto doubted ultimate victory in a war with the United States. Taking a hard look at his chances, Yamamoto prophesied he would "run wild" for six months. The outcome after that was uncertain, and absolute victory would be achieved only with "a capitulation at the White House, in Washington itself. I wonder if whether the politicians of the day really have the willingness to make the sacrifices, and the confidence, that this would entail?" A move to "decide the fate of the war on the very first day" inspired Yamamoto to try a knockout blow at Pearl Harbor.

The concept of a devastating surprise attack at Pearl Harbor was not a new idea. During a joint Army-Navy exercise in 1932, aircraft from USS *Saratoga* and *Lexington* swept in from the sea to launch a surprise morning "attack" on Sunday, 7 February. Observing aerial torpedo exercises in the spring of 1940, Yamamoto whispered to Rear Admiral Shigeru Fukudome, "I wonder if an aerial attack can't be made at Pearl Harbor." The U.S. exercise, the talent of the Japanese pilots, and the British success against the Italian fleet anchored in shallow waters at Taranto in 1940 firmed Yamamoto's resolve, and he ordered a young tactical genius of aerial warfare, Commander Minoru Genda, to begin operational planning. The plan, agreed to after months of disagreement among the ranks of command in the Japanese Navy, called for high-altitude bombings, aerial torpedo attacks, and strafing runs on Oahu's airfields and the U.S. Navy's ships. Submarines, including five of the Navy's Type A two-man midgets, were to participate, attacking the fleet inside the harbor and catching any ships that got to sea. When negotiations with the United States were deemed unlikely to continue to the satisfaction of the Tojo government, the Navy asked for and received

Imperial blessing on 6 September 1941 for its "Hawaii Operation." Japan was thus fully committed to war after nearly a year of preparation.

A twenty-eight–vessel "kido butai," or strike force, was assembled on Tankan Bay in Northern Japan under the command of Vice Admiral Chuichi Nagumo. Sailing in secrecy on 26 November, the task force made its way to Hawaii without detection.

Arriving on position two hundred miles north of Oahu early on the morning of 7 December, Hawaii time, the carriers *Akagi*, *Kaga*, *Hiryu*, *Soryu*, *Shokaku*, and *Zuikaku* launched two waves of high-altitude bombers, torpedo bombers, dive-bombers, and fighters. At 7:55 A.M. Hawaii time, the first wave, under Commander Mitsuo Fuchida, hit Pearl Harbor and Hickam, Ewa, Wheeler, and Kaneohe fields, catching the Army, Navy, and Marine Corps forces off guard. The second wave, under Lieutenant Commander Shigeru Shimazaki, struck Bellows Airfield, Kaneohe and Hickam fields,

and Pearl Harbor approximately one hour later at 8:50. Japanese torpedoes, bombs, and projectiles slammed into ships, aircraft, and men, wreaking a terrible toll. When the attack was finally over and the last plane, Fuchida's, departed at 9:32, the Japanese left behind 2,403 dead or missing and 1,178 wounded Americans. Eight battleships, three light cruisers, three destroyers, and four auxiliary craft were either damaged, capsized, or sunk, while 162 aircraft were destroyed and 159 were damaged. More than half of the dead were from the battleship *Arizona*. Of the approximately 1,500 men in the crew, only about 300 survived. Japanese losses were light—twenty-nine planes, with fifty-five airmen, and five midget submarines, with ten crew members, lost during the attack and an I-class submarine sunk in the aftermath of the attack.

The raid of 7 December galvanized the United States into furious response. As news of Pearl Harbor was broadcast to the nation on an otherwise quiet Sunday, the formerly isolationist mood of America shifted to war. Franklin D. Roosevelt, speaking before Congress, asked for a declaration of war against Japan for its actions on "a day which will live in infamy."

The declaration of war marked the United States' grim determination to win an unconditional surrender from Japan. Inspired by the popular slogan "Remember Pearl Harbor!" the United States began a massive salvage of the Pacific Fleet and pushed its industrial capacity to build the ships, planes, and weapons needed for the years of fighting ahead, against not only Japan but also Japan's Axis partners, Germany and Italy. Part of the inspiration for the fight came from the tremendous heroism that the American defenders of Oahu displayed on 7 December. Six Medals of Honor, fifty-one Navy Crosses, fifty-three Silver Stars, four Navy and Marine Corps medals, four Distinguished Service Crosses, three Bronze Stars, and a Distinguished Flying Cross were among the awards for heroism and sacrifice, along with numerous commendations.

Yamamoto's fear that the Japanese had "awakened a sleeping giant, and filled him with a terrible resolve" was realized. Four of the six attacking carriers—*Akagi*, *Kaga*, *Hiryu*, and *Soryu*—were sunk in combat at Midway just six months after the attack on Pearl Harbor. After months of "running wild," the Imperial Japanese Navy, and in turn its Army and government, were in retreat. Four years of submarine warfare, carrier strikes, fierce sea battles, amphibious assaults, and bloody hand-to-hand island combat would wrest Japanese-held territories and even the home waters from Japan. Throughout the war, ships and submarines leaving Pearl Harbor would steam past the shattered hulk of *Arizona* to wreak a terrible vengeance and defeat the Japanese on land and sea.

Pearl Harbor Recalled

The Paintings

Many Americans, including those of us too young to remember the fateful events of 7 December 1941, are nonetheless familiar with the images of Pearl Harbor that photographers captured at the time of the stunning Japanese attack. The tilted foremast of USS *Arizona*, wreathed in thick black smoke—the arching trails of fire and debris as USS *Shaw*'s magazines exploded—the damaged destroyers *Cassin* and *Downes* and the battleship *Pennsylvania* in the flooded and fire-scarred Dry Dock No. 1—all are famous, oft-published scenes of the day of infamy. Yet these images are of the aftermath of the battle. Few scenes exist of men, ships, and airplanes in action—a blurry image of three Vals diving at *Nevada,* captured Japanese aerial photographs of geysers of water shooting up from Battleship Row and of shock waves and gushing oil spreading from ruptured hulls. These join the grainy images taken at a distance of the tremendous fireball erupting at the moment of *Arizona*'s violent death. Captured imperfectly on film and for the most part in black and white, and shot in the midst of excitement and horror, these photographs barely begin to match the countless other images never graphically expressed but nonetheless indelibly etched in the minds of the survivors and recounted in verbal and written descriptions.

Tom Freeman, working from the available accounts—including hours of interviews and oral histories taken from those who were there, the latest scholarship from both sides, and archaeological evidence discerned from the study of the shattered wreckage of *Arizona* in recent years—has in this collection presented his interpretation of the otherwise graphically undocumented images of 7 December 1941. His paintings provide in sharp detail and vivid color a comprehensive view of the attack on Pearl Harbor, from the massing of the Japanese strike force and the launching of aircraft and midget submarines to the splashing of planes, the torpedoing of *Oklahoma*, the gallant run of *Nevada* for the open sea, the spraying down of *Arizona*'s burning hulk by a Navy tug, and the arrival of the B-17s at Hickam Field.

More than merely capturing the image, Freeman has also placed the viewer in close proximity to the action. You are next to *Arizona* as it explodes, tons of powder and fuel oil creating a fireball that tears through bulkheads, lifts decks straight into the air, and pushes out the casemates that line the bow. You can feel the clammy cold of a half-flooded compartment lit by a battle lantern, the blistering heat of fuel-stoked fires burning out of control, and the concussion that shakes steel plates and wire rigging as a torpedo strikes home. The paintings are that forcefully immediate.

The paintings in the Pearl Harbor collection are

published here for the fiftieth anniversary of the attack so that future generations can compare the visual images with the written and tape-recorded memories of those who served and fought on that never-to-be-forgotten Sunday morning. The collection begins with a vignette of Pearl Harbor just before the attack. The paintings are arranged in rough chronological order, beginning with Japanese drills to perfect shallow-water aerial torpedo attack, which was a critical aspect of the "Hawaii Operation," and then follow the Imperial Japanese Navy as it sorties, crosses the Pacific, and launches its strike.

Other paintings illustrate the participation of the midget submarines, the attacks on the Army, Navy, and Marine Corps airfields, and the devastating assault on the fleet at Pearl Harbor. The futility of the American response, be it the firing of a .45 at enemy planes or an attempted takeoff through a Japanese strafing attack, is matched by the heroic flight of Lieutenants Welch and Taylor as they dogfight with the Japanese, or by the courage of those who saved men and equipment so that they could fight another day.

The chronological presentation ends at sunset on 7 December, when two young officers from *Arizona* lower the flag from the fantail of their shattered battleship. A special epilogue recounts the story of *Arizona*, now the focal point of the *Arizona* Memorial and the subject of a recent five-year archaeological study, as well as other ships. The final painting shows *Arizona*'s submerged remains, which rest beneath Pearl Harbor like a frozen moment of time, battle damage yet visible, still leaking oil from its ruptured bunkers.

The Final Moments of Peace: The U.S. Pacific Fleet on the Morning of 7 December 1941

Ninety-seven vessels were anchored or moored at Pearl Harbor on the morning of 7 December 1941, and there were sixty-four more ships within three miles of Oahu, according to the research of the Pearl Harbor History Associates. The best known were the capital ships. Seven battleships—*Arizona, Nevada, West Virginia, Oklahoma, Maryland, Tennessee,* and *California*—were moored along Battleship Row, and one—*Pennsylvania*—was in dry dock. Two heavy and six light cruisers, three of which—*Helena, Honolulu,* and *Raleigh*—were damaged in the attack, were there. Moored near the Aloha Tower on the Honolulu waterfront was the Coast Guard cutter *Taney*. The largest number of ships of any one type was thirty destroyers. Three were heavily damaged—*Cassin, Downes,* and *Shaw*.

The fleet included twenty-four minecraft, whose flagship, *Oglala,* was sunk. Three auxiliaries, including the target ship and former battleship *Utah,* were in the harbor with four submarines, six airplane tenders, a sub tender, three seaplane derricks, and six net vessels. Other smaller vessels included twelve PT boats en route with *Ramapo* to the Philippines, a yard-patrol boat, two destroyer tenders, a sub-rescue vessel, a gunboat, two ferryboats, three water barges, a torpedo test barge, and three repair ships, including *Vestal*, whose commanding officer, Cassin Young, would earn the Medal of Honor for his actions. There were also two oilers, an ammunition ship, three fleet tugs, three stores ships, a hospital ship—*Solace*—and nine yard tugs, including *Hoga*, whose crew would distinguish itself by assisting the crippled *Nevada* and *Oglala* and extinguishing the fires on *Arizona*. Three garbage lighters and two repair barges added to the number of more humble craft at Pearl Harbor. Of these ships and craft, five were damaged or lost—the seaplane tender *Curtiss*; the tug *Sotoyomo*, the oldest ship present, having been built in

1903; *Utah*; the repair ship *Vestal*, at that time the ship at Pearl in commission the longest, with nearly thirty-two years to its credit; and YFD-2.

Of all these ships and craft, only three were not completely salvaged—*Arizona*, *Utah*, and *Oklahoma*. In the years that followed, sixteen ships made famous at Pearl Harbor on 7 December 1941 were also lost, among them *Ward*, which fired the first shot; *Monaghan*, which rammed and sank an attacking Japanese midget submarine in the harbor; and the tanker *Neosho*, which miraculously escaped the attack.

Other Pearl Harbor ships that survived the war lasted through the decades, the last Navy ship to serve ending its naval career in May 1973 when the tug *Nokomis* (YT-142) retired. The last survivor to go out of commission was USCGC *Taney*, decommissioned, appropriately enough, on 7 December 1986.

In this comprehensive, three-dimensional view of Pearl Harbor on the fateful morning of 7 December 1941, the Pacific Fleet lies at anchor, with some ships about to get underway. It is 7:45 in the morning. The first wave of the Japanese strike force is just off Oahu. There are ten minutes of peace left for the ships, sailors, marines, and soldiers on the island.

Phase I of the Attack: A concentrated attack by perhaps sixty-six torpedo bombers, dive-bombers, and horizontal bombers lasted from 7:55 to 8:25 A.M.

Phase II of the Attack: About fifteen dive-bombers conducted sporadic attacks from 8:25 to 8:40 A.M.

Phase III of the Attack: An estimated forty-eight horizontal bombers launched a heavy attack that lasted from 8:40 to 9:15 A.M.

Phase IV of the Attack: About twenty-seven dive-bombers conducted strafing attacks from 9:15 to 9:45 A.M.

Phase V of the Attack: All Japanese planes left the scene and returned to their carriers.

The First Carrier Division Perfects Shallow-Water Aerial Torpedo Attacks at Kagoshima, November 1941

The key to success at Pearl Harbor, as far as Admiral Yamamoto was concerned, lay in the ability of his pilots to perform what was in 1940 an impossible feat. When Yamamoto decided that the Imperial Japanese Navy would initiate a war with the United States in an aerial attack, he knew that a critical aspect of the operation would be an assault by carrier-based planes with torpedoes. But conventional aerial torpedo attacks dropped the weapons deep, at times as much as a hundred feet beneath the surface. The destructive power of these explosive-tipped steel lances was unleashed only after they had run a long distance to arm. Pearl Harbor was narrow and confined, so the torpedoes would not have time to arm. The harbor was also too shallow—forty feet deep at the maximum—and torpedoes dropped into it would stick in the muddy bottom.

As operational planning for the attack progressed,

high-altitude and strafing attacks by other planes were added to the shaky if not impossible task of the torpedo bombers. The concept of an aerial torpedo attack was never abandoned, however, for the Japanese had been, as historian Gordon Prange would later note, leaders in aerial-torpedo-attack techniques since 1933. The successful assault by British torpedo planes against the Italian fleet anchored at Taranto on 12 November 1940 argued for pressing forward with an aerial torpedo assault on the U.S. Pacific Fleet, and in early June 1941 the First Carrier Division began training for such an attack.

The B5N2 Kates drilled incessantly through the summer and fall of 1941 and shattered the peace of Kagoshima, whose bay lies on the southeastern shore of Kyushu. The pilots practiced low-altitude approaches and torpedo runs, at times barely skimming over the water, hoping to achieve a maximum torpedo depth of thirty-three feet.

Technicians ashore tackled another problem. An important part of the program lay in stabilizing the Model II torpedoes so that they would run shallow and straight. Fins attached to the tails of the torpedoes resolved the problem, as did altering the fuzes to arm at much shorter distances. The Mitsubishi plant in Nagasaki produced a batch of specially modified torpedoes at breakneck speed. The first arrived at Kagoshima on 30 October, with more arriving by 4 November 1941 for final testing.

The torpedoes, married with the new method of attack, proved successful. Coming in over land and passing the city of Kagoshima, the pilots dropped low and level over the water, at a 100-knot speed, and let go the torpedoes, which 82 percent of the time ran shallow and true toward the target buoy moored offshore. News of the final triumph of the torpedo bombers was received just a few days prior to the completion of the last batch of specially modified torpedoes on 17 November.

The final batch was loaded on the carrier *Kaga* at Sasebo on 18 November. *Kaga* sailed on the 19th to rendezvous with the other carriers and distribute the torpedoes.

Forty Kates climbed into the skies off Oahu on the morning of 7 December, and the torpedoes they carried and the constant training of the pilots who flew them paid off for the Japanese, for the torpedoes would slash through the water to tear into ships' vitals with deadly effect.

Sixty feet above the water a Nakajima B5N2 Kate looses a specially modified Model II torpedo in a practice run on Kagoshima Bay.

The Gathering Storm: The Japanese Fleet Sorties from Tankan Bay

Preparations for the attack on Pearl Harbor were made in absolute secrecy. After training was completed in mid-November, the strike force for the "Hawaii Operation," as the attack was called, sailed singly to the Kuriles, a chain of volcanic islands stretching north from Hokkaido, where they rendezvoused at Tankan Bay on Etorofu Island. The carrier *Kaga*, carrying the torpedoes that had been specially modified for the attack, was the last to arrive.

After the task force assembled in the cold, wind-whipped waters of the Kuriles, Admiral Yamamoto issued the operational order to Vice Admiral Nagumo: "The Task Force will leave Tankan Bay on 26 November, and making every effort to conceal its movement, advance to the standby point, where fueling will be quickly completed." On the dark and cloudy morning of the 26th, the fleet raised anchor and steamed from the bay into the North Pacific. As Lieutenant Commander

Fuchida, who was aboard *Akagi,* later recalled,

The sortie was cloaked in complete secrecy. A patrol boat guarding the bay entrance flashed a message, "Good luck on your mission." But even that boat was unaware of our assignment. The *Akagi* signalled "Thanks," and passed by, her ensign fluttering in the breeze. ... the crews shouted "Banzai!" as they took what might be their last look at Japan. ... Sitting at the flight deck control post under the bridge, I watched the gradually receding mountains of the Kuriles. The young men of the flying crews were boiling over with fighting spirit. Hard nights and days of training had been followed by hasty preparations, and now the sortie, which meant that they were going to war.

With a Kawanishi H8K Flying Boat passing overhead, the carrier Soryu *steams out of Tankan Bay, past a patrol boat, as the Pearl Harbor strike force sorties on the cold, grey morning of 26 November 1941.*

Across a "Vacant Sea," *Akagi* Steams to Pearl Harbor

The Pearl Harbor strike force that sortied from Tankan Bay was formidable. The heart of the "kido butai" was six aircraft carriers—*Kaga, Akagi, Hiryu, Soryu, Shokaku,* and *Zuikaku*. The battleships *Hiei* and *Kirishima,* the heavy cruisers *Chikuma* and *Tone,* the light cruiser *Abukuma,* nine destroyers, and three I-class submarines screened and protected the carriers. Nine tankers sailed with the fleet to refuel them at sea. The carriers brought 350 aircraft for the attack—79 Mitsubishi A6M2 Type 21 Reisen Zero fighters, 143 Nakajima B5N2 Kate torpedo/horizontal bombers, and 128 Aichi D3A1 Type 99 Val carrier dive-bombers. The planes were armed with 7.7-mm and 20-mm machine guns, the specially modified Type II torpedoes, 250-kilogram and 60-kilogram bombs, and 16.1-inch shells from the battleships *Nagato* and *Mutsu* modified into high-altitude, armor-piercing shells.

Nagumo flew his flag as Commander-in-Chief First

Air Fleet from *Akagi*. With him on the carrier sailed Minoru Genda, the man who had planned much of the attack, and Fuchida, the leader of the first assault wave. *Akagi*, besides being flagship, carried part of the assault wave—eighteen Reisen Zero fighters, eighteen Aichi Val dive-bombers, and twenty-seven Nakajima Kate bombers.

Reaching Pearl Harbor without being detected by merchant ships at sea, or worse yet by American patrols, was critical. At night, a strict blackout was ordered, and radio silence was observed. For the first half of the voyage, a quarter of the force was constantly at battle stations; at the half-way point, half the force went to battle stations. Additionally, six Zero fighters on each carrier were kept constantly ready. The Japanese were lucky as they sailed through what historian Gordon Prange would later describe as "the vacant sea." The route selected bore east for eight days before turning southeast and heading for Oahu on 4 December, Japan time. Although stormy weather and fog screened the task force, the rough seas made refueling dangerous: fuel lines occasionally snapped, sweeping men overboard.

On 2 December the fleet was irrevocably committed to conflict. The signal "Niitaka Yama Nobore" or "Climb Mount Niitaka" was sent to Nagumo, authorizing him to attack. The task force was then due north of Midway Island. On the morning of 7 December, Japan time, the fleet, then six hundred miles north of Oahu, refueled one final time. The attacking force then closed on the Hawaiian Islands at 24 knots, arriving in position 230 miles out, where the planes would launch before dawn.

Shrouded in fog, the carrier Akagi *slices through the cold North Pacific waters en route to Pearl Harbor while Japan's negotiations with the United States move inexorably toward war.*

The American Carriers Miss the Attack: USS *Lexington* (CV-2) Sails

The U.S. Navy received funds in 1920 to convert the collier *Jupiter* (AC-3) into an aircraft carrier. Conversion of the collier into a hybrid ship at the Norfolk Navy Yard took two years, and it was relaunched on 22 March 1922 as USS *Langley* (CV-1), the U.S. Navy's first aircraft carrier.

At that time, the Navy also planned to convert the incomplete cruisers *Lexington* and *Saratoga* into fully functional fleet carriers. Authorized in 1916 as part of a three-year program of naval construction, "Lady Lex" was laid down as the lead cruiser of the six-vessel *Lexington* class. But postwar conferences, conventions, and treaties limited the number of battleships and cruisers, the world's most powerful weapons. Under the terms of the treaty signed as a result of the Washington Naval Conference of 1921–22, battleships and battle cruisers then under construction could be scrapped, or in the case of two vessels per signatory nation, converted to aircraft carriers. Japan chose to convert the battleship *Kaga* and the battle cruiser *Akagi* to fleet carriers. Ironically, Japanese anger over the naval arms limitations imposed by the treaty was a contributing factor in the coming war.

Lexington and *Saratoga* were rebuilt as carriers (CV-2 and CV-3, respectively). The first fleet carriers of the Navy, they were major successes, spending their prewar careers in fleet training exercises that defined a strong role for aircraft carriers in naval warfare. These exercises included staged "attacks" on the Panama Canal and Pearl Harbor. The successful "attack" on Pearl Harbor in February 1932 received much attention after 7 December 1941.

The U.S. carrier force was a prime target of the "Hawaii Operation", but it alone survived intact. While the Japanese had more carriers than the United States, the U.S. ships were superior vessels. Even the oldest of the fleet carriers, *Saratoga* and *Lexington*, were faster and handled more planes than the Japanese carriers. The departure of the *Yorktown* (CV-5) on 20 April 1941 for the Atlantic Fleet had removed one potential threat to Japan. Fortunately for the United States, the three remaining fleet carriers in the Pacific missed the attack. *Enterprise* (CV-6), nicknamed the "Big E," sailed to Wake Island to deliver aircraft on 28 November and was due back on the 7th of December. *Saratoga* was in California, entering San Diego harbor after an overhaul at the Puget Sound Navy Yard in Bremerton, Washington. *Lexington* sailed from Pearl Harbor for Midway on 5 December.

The "Big E" was close to Pearl Harbor on the 7th, and Vice Admiral William F. Halsey, aboard the carrier, dispatched planes to Pearl that were caught up in the aftermath of the Japanese attack, dogfighting with the enemy. Some of *Enterprise*'s planes were even shot down by jittery American gunners. When *Enterprise* entered

Pearl Harbor on the afternoon of the 8th and steamed slowly past the smoking, burning, and sunken hulks of the Pacific Fleet's battle line, Halsey muttered, "Before we're through with 'em, the Japanese language will be spoken only in hell."

The veteran carrier Lexington *sails from Pearl Harbor on 5 December. One of the prime targets of the Japanese assault, "Lady Lex" unwittingly escapes the attack.*

Arizona's Last Portrait

USS *Arizona* (BB-39) was the third U.S. warship to bear that name. Laid down at the New York Navy Yard and launched there on 19 June 1915, *Arizona* was named for the territory that had recently become the forty-eighth state. Commissioned on 17 October 1916, the battleship, the second and last of the *Pennsylvania* class, joined the U.S. Atlantic Fleet in time for the U.S. entry into the First World War. *Arizona* did not see action in that conflict, however, because it was employed in training in both the Chesapeake Bay and the Atlantic, and at anchor much of the time in the York River off Yorktown, Virginia.

The battleship was ordered to British waters following the cessation of hostilities in 1918. There, on 12 December 1918, it steamed from Portsmouth, England, to Brest, France, as part of the escort for President Woodrow Wilson, who was aboard *George Washington*. Following this duty, *Arizona* returned to the United

States, crossing the Atlantic once again in early 1919 to cruise the Mediterranean for a few months. Returning to the United States in July 1919, *Arizona* served an uneventful career with the Atlantic Fleet, cruising the Atlantic coast of the United States and the Caribbean.

In 1921 the battleship was sent into the Pacific to join the U.S. Pacific Fleet. It remained with the Pacific Fleet until the end of its career, with a three-year break in service when it returned to the Atlantic coast to undergo modernization under the naval appropriations of 1929–31. Before rejoining the Pacific Fleet in 1931, *Arizona* carried President Herbert C. Hoover on a cruise to the West Indies. The battleship steamed to San Diego in August 1931, but it made a visit to New York in 1934 and last left the Atlantic on 24 October 1934.

As flagship of Battleship Division One, *Arizona* hosted Rear Admiral Chester W. Nimitz from 1938 to 1939. Nimitz was succeeded as commander of the

Battleship Division by Russell Willson, who was relieved by Isaac Kidd in January 1941.

The battleship moved with the other vessels of the Pacific Fleet to Pearl Harbor on Oahu in April 1940, when it was decided to shift the home port from San Diego. *Arizona* sailed back to the West Coast at the end of 1940, where it underwent an overhaul at Bremerton before returning to Pearl Harbor in February. The ship visited California once more, leaving San Pedro for the last time on 1 July 1941. The *Arizona*'s next months were often spent at sea, participating in intensive battle-readiness drills. Mock air attacks launched from *Enterprise* helped sharpen the skills of the battleship's gunners as the threat of war grew imminent.

Cruising off Oahu, Arizona *passes Diamond Head in consort with a four-stacker. Two PBYs pass overhead, watching the battleship as it maneuvers on its last battle-readiness drill on 5 December 1941.*

ARIZONA

Tom Freeman
©1990

I-24 Launches Midget Submarine *HA-19*

Initially conceived as an aerial assault, the attack on Pearl Harbor was modified to combat test the Imperial Japanese Navy's small fleet of midget submarines. The midgets, known as "A-hyoteki" or "A-targets," were the inspiration of Captain Kaneji Kishimoto, IJN. The seventy-eight-foot long, forty-six-ton, two-man craft were propelled by battery-powered motors. Although conceived in 1934, the first midgets were not built until 1936. Construction of forty-nine "Type A" midgets followed at Kure and Ourazaki in 1938, and by mid-1941 submarines *HA-3* through *HA-52* were ready for combat.

In October 1941 the crews of the midgets were ordered to train for assaults on Pearl Harbor and Singapore while five I-class boats of the First Submarine Squadron of the Sixth Submarine Fleet were modified to carry a midget on the deck aft of the sail. Doubts about the role of the midgets, particularly the fear that they might prematurely attack and sound the alarm for the

Americans, plagued Japanese planners, and as late as 14 November the decision to include the midgets had not been made. The order was finally given, and on 18 November five submarines—*I-16*, *I-18*, *I-20*, *I-22*, and *I-24*—sailed in secrecy from Kure for Oahu. Designated the "Special Attack Force," the midgets were ordered to slip covertly into the harbor, wait until the attack began, and then surface and launch torpedoes. The midgets would then navigate submerged, counterclockwise around Ford Island, to escape and rendezvous with the mother submarines seven miles off Lanai Island.

Reaching their destination on 5 December, the five submarines fanned out, closing to within ten miles of Diamond Head to wait. On 7 December the five submarines, their hulls covered with algae and slippery green moss, rose from the depths in the predawn darkness. Below decks, the midget submariners ate a good-luck meal of red rice and prepared for action.

The first midget launched from *I-16* at midnight. The others followed, and at 3:30 A.M. the last midget, *I-24*'s, was ready for launching. Midget *HA-19*, commanded by Ensign Kazuo Sakamaki and Chief Warrant Officer Kiyoshi Inagaki, had been plagued with problems. The small craft's gyrocompass was out of order despite Sakamaki's frantic attempts to repair it. As the time for launching approached, *I-24*'s captain, Lieutenant Commander Hiroshi Hanabusa, asked Sakamaki what he intended to do. "We will go," Sakamaki declared firmly, and he and Hanbusa shouted, "On to Pearl Harbor!" As *I-24* bobbed on the surface, the lights of Honolulu in the distance, Sakamaki and Inagaki, stripping down to fundoshi and wearing leather jackets and hachimaki, climbed out on deck and ascended the hull of their craft. The submarine's crew bade them an emotional farewell.

In the predawn darkness, I-24 rides in the swell off Oahu. The crew of midget submarine HA-19 clambers up its slippery, glistening wet hull.

"We Have Attacked, Fired Upon and Dropped Depth Charges Upon Submarine Operating in Defensive Sea Area"

At 3:42 A.M., one and three-quarter miles south of the Pearl Harbor entrance buoys, the minesweeper USS *Condor* spotted the periscope of a submerged submarine making straight for it at 9 knots. As the periscope suddenly veered away, the minesweeper notified the defensive-area patrol destroyer, USS *Ward* (DD-139), of the sighting by blinker. The destroyer searched the defensive zone without success until 4:35, when the vintage four stacker's commander, Lieutenant William Outerbridge, secured the ship from general quarters.

Little more than an hour later, the stores and supply ship *Antares* slowly approached the entrance to Pearl Harbor, passing the Barbers Point Light at 5:45. From his vantage on the bridge, Commander Lawrence C. Grannis, the ship's commanding officer, watched the sun come up. Looking behind his ship at the lighter he was towing, Grannis' gaze suddenly stopped. Following

Antares was a strange submarine, obviously struggling to submerge. Grannis contacted Outerbridge on *Ward* and asked the destroyer to investigate.

As *Ward* charged forward, Ensign William Tanner, at the controls of a PBY on routine morning patrol above the harbor, also spotted the submarine. Dropping two smoke pots near the submarine to guide *Ward* to what Tanner assumed was an American fleet boat in distress, the PBY banked off at 6:33. Four minutes later Outerbridge sighted the vessel, which was making 12 knots in a direct run for the harbor entrance. It was not an American submarine.

Outerbridge had distinct orders to attack any submarine operating in the defensive area. Sounding general quarters at 6:40, *Ward* surged ahead as sleepy crewmen scrambled from their bunks to man the guns. The crew of No. 1 gun was ready first and at 6:45 fired a 4-inch shell that passed over the submarine's exposed conning tower. The crew of the No. 3 gun fired from their position in the waist. The submarine was only fifty yards off now, and closing. The shell hit at the junction of the conning tower and the pressure hull. The midget heeled over to starboard, slowed, and sank at 6:46. The U.S. Navy, which had traded shots with German U-Boats in the Atlantic and had probably sunk one, had just made its first confirmed kill of World War II.

The opening shots of the war preceded the air attack by an hour. Outerbridge radioed a report that he had depth charged the submarine at 6:51, amending the message at 6:53 to read, "We have attacked, fired upon and dropped depth charges upon submarine operating in defensive sea area." Headquarters did not heed the importance of the destroyer's sinking of a submarine in the defensive zone until it was too late. As Admiral Kimmel was notified of *Ward*'s action, Japanese planes closed to strike at an unsuspecting fleet at anchor.

As the destroyer surges ahead at full speed, the crew of the No. 4 gun prepares to ram home a 4-inch shell. **Ward's** *target, visible above the surface aft of the supply ship* **Antares,** *is the conning tower of a midget submarine, highlighted against the spray of the near miss from the No. 1 gun.*

"Enemy Fleet in Port": *Chikuma*'s Scout Plane Climbs into the Morning Skies off Oahu

At 5:30 A.M. the pilots, observers, and wireless operators of two Aichi 13A1 Jake floatplanes climbed into their aircraft on board the heavy cruisers *Chikuma* and *Tone*. From across the water came the roaring of airplane engines as the strike force on the carriers warmed up for the assault. Catapulted from the cruisers' pitching and rolling decks into the darkness of the predawn sky, the planes split up, *Chikuma*'s heading for Pearl Harbor and *Tone*'s for Lahaina Anchorage on the island of Maui. The submarine *I-72* had scouted the deep-water anchorage at Lahaina the day before without sighting the U.S. fleet, but Admiral Nagumo was ensuring that his strike force would not miss the American ships.

The floatplanes were single-engine, three-man craft with cruising speeds of 120 knots and ranges of 1,298 nautical miles. As they sped off to determine the whereabouts of the Pacific Fleet and assess the weather, there was some consternation on the nearby carriers because some thought the two Jakes were enemy planes. However, they were quickly identified, to the relief of those who feared discovery by American scouts.

U.S. radar probably spotted the planes as they flew toward the Hawaiian Islands, but no alarm was raised. The floatplanes reached their destinations at the same time. Ordered not to overfly the targets but to circle five miles off, *Tone*'s plane signaled that Lahaina was empty. *Chikuma*'s plane followed with a transmission at 7:33, reporting clouds at 1,700 meters over the harbor and winds of 14 knots. The most important part of the Jake's message, however, was the report, "Enemy Fleet in port," although the aircrew miscounted ten battleships, a heavy cruiser, and ten light cruisers at anchor.

The first wave of the strike force, led by Commander Fuchida, was close behind the floatplanes, having launched soon after they had flown off. Minutes after the Jakes had reported, the Japanese attack planes deployed off Kahuku Point before splitting to hit their assigned targets. The first bombs fell eight minutes later.

A Jake float plane climbs into the sky after being catapulted from the pitching deck of the heavy cruiser Chikuma. *The Jake will fly to Oahu ahead of the soon-to-be-launched strike force to make sure that the American fleet is in port.*

TomFreeman
© 1990

Fuchida Launches from *Akagi* with the First Wave

The six carriers of the strike force moved into launch position in the early morning hours of 7 December. Maintenance crews worked through the night to ready the aircraft, and after 1:00 A.M. the screening and escort ships of the task force could hear the roar of airplane engines warming up on the carriers' decks.

Fuchida rose at 5:00 and dressed in his flight suit. For this occasion he added red long johns and a red shirt, so that if he was wounded the blood would not alarm his pilots. After a quick breakfast, Fuchida, Admiral Nagumo, and *Akagi*'s captain, Kiichi Hasegawa, joined the pilots for a final briefing. Fuchida was confident of success, but Admiral Nagumo was worried, despite his expressions of confidence. His carriers were only 230 miles off Oahu, well within the range of American patrols.

At 6:00 the briefing ended, and the pilots scrambled to their planes. Because of the rough seas, the ships pitched and rolled in the predawn darkness. A brisk wind whipped across the flight deck as the battle ensign was hoisted, followed by a signal famous in Japanese naval history, the "Z" flag flown by Admiral Togo as he steamed into victory against the Russian fleet during the Battle of Tsushima in May 1905. *Akagi* surged east at 24 knots, facing into the wind.

The fighters launched first. Lieutenant Commander Shigeru Itaya's Zero rolled forward with the pitch of the deck, roared off the edge, and dropped sharply, but then climbed into the sky. The other fighters followed, and then came the high-altitude bombers under Fuchida's direct command. Around his helmet Fuchida wore a white hachimaki, a special gift from the maintenance crew. To the cheers of the flight crew, Fuchida roared down the flight deck and lifted into the sky.

The other carriers launched at the same time, and within fifteen minutes the planes of the first wave had rendezvoused, heading toward Oahu at 6:15. As they neared the island, the rising sun's rays stretched out of the clouds and struck the water in a graphic reminder of the Japanese naval ensign. It was an auspicious omen, and Fuchida rolled back his canopy, stood at attention, and then proudly gazed back at the 183 planes that surrounded him.

At 7:40 the thick cloud cover broke as the planes reached Kahuku Point at Oahu's northern shore. It was time for deployment, and the planes swept to the west around the point. Fuchida again opened his canopy and fired a single shot with his flare pistol, the signal to proceed with a surprise attack. Nine minutes later, Fuchida could see Pearl Harbor ahead of and below him, still unaware of the Japanese approach. Turning to his radioman at 7:50, he ordered a signal to be sent to the other planes in the attack formation. The radioman rapped out the message in Morse: "To, To, To… ."

The fighters and bombers separated, climbing to various altitudes or swooping down on Oahu. At 7:55 bullets smacked into parked aircraft at Hickam Field, and two minutes later the first bombs fell on Battleship Row. As smoke and flame climbed into the pale morning sky, Fuchida sent another signal back to the fleet, the prearranged code for a successful surprise attack, "Tora, Tora, Tora."

Freak atmospheric conditions allowed the signal to bounce across the Pacific to Hiroshima Bay. There it was received in the radio room of the battleship *Nagato,* where an anxious Yamamoto awaited word. The admiral who planned and pushed for the attack then knew that the war in the Pacific had begun in Japan's favor.

As a stiff wind whips the flags flying from Akagi's *masthead, Commander Fuchida's Nakajima Kate rolls forward to launch amidst the cheers and waves of the carrier's crew.*

"Well, Don't Worry about It": Tracking Incoming Planes at Opana

The practical use of radar as an instrument of war was in its infancy in 1940. Nonetheless, the new technology, although at times erratic, was better than the existing "antiair system" at protecting the fleet.

On 24 January 1941 Secretary of the Navy Frank Knox, acting on the suggestions of his officers, wrote Secretary of War Henry Stimson with recommendations for bolstering the security of the fleet at Pearl Harbor. Knox was upset because security from air attack rested entirely on a few patrol planes, "visual observation and sound locators which are only effective up to four miles." The situation would be better by mid-summer 1941, noted Stimson, when additional planes, antiaircraft guns, and "radio locators" with "an effective range of 100 miles" would arrive.

Temporary radar installations, mobile 270-B sets mounted on van-type trucks, were sent to Hawaii. Mobile radar sites were established at Koko Head,

Kaawa, Kawailoa, Opana, and Fort Shafter. These primitive units broadcast brief, intense pulses of radio waves that sped out at the speed of light (186,000 miles per second), reflected off a target, and then sped back to the receiving set, where the signal appeared as a "pip" on the cathode-ray-tube screen. Although the range of the sets was rated at 100 miles, they could reach out to 150 miles.

The army manned these units of the aircraft warning service. The lack of experience with the new technology and erratic readings led to a few false alarms, but gradually the army operators grew accustomed to their sets, some by dint of hard practice.

On 7 December Privates Joseph E. Lockard and George E. Elliott, assigned to the Opana station at Kahuku Point, rose from their tent at 3:45 A.M., fired up their set, and reported for duty on schedule at 4:00. The third member of the radar team, the operator of the generator, did not show up for duty, but the two privates took his place as motor man and began to sweep the skies north of Oahu. Occasional pips appeared on the screen at around 6:45, increasing for the next five to ten minutes. The stations at Kaawa and Kawailoa also picked up pips, which they relayed by phone to the plotting station at the information center at Fort Shafter. They were probably tracking the scouting aircraft launched from the *Chikuma*.

The duty hours for each station ended at 7:00, but Elliot and Lockard stayed to get a little more practice. It was then that Opana picked up a big pip, indicating a mass of aircraft, perhaps fifty planes or more, approaching from the north, 136 miles out. As the pip came closer, the men phoned their report in to Fort Shafter, which had also closed down at the end of the shift. Lockard spoke to Lieutenant Kermit Tyler, the only officer left at the information center, who, believing

Opana was tracking the incoming B-17s from Hamilton Field, told him, "Well, don't worry about it."

When he hung up, Lockard saw that Elliott was continuing to track the incoming planes, which, by 7:15, were eighty-eight miles away. For the practice, Elliott kept at his scope until 7:39, when he lost the pip because of interference from the surrounding mountains. The planes were then only twenty-two miles away.

By the time Elliot and Lockard shut down the set and climbed into a truck at 7:45 to drive to Kawailoa, where they lived, the first wave of the strike force had already spotted Kahuku Point and deployed into attack position. Had the two men remained a few minutes more, they might even have spotted the Japanese formation as it roared past Kahuku and swept west toward Kaena Point.

Approaching Kawailoa at 7:55, Elliott and Lockard watched mutely as plumes of smoke rose from the direction of Pearl Harbor. The import of their sighting came home in a chilling fashion. It had indeed been something to worry about.

In the predawn darkness, Privates Lockard and Elliot report for duty at the mobile radar station at Opana Point. The primitive radar set, sweeping the skies off Oahu for approaching aircraft, will register the incoming wave of Japanese planes.

Havoc at Wheeler

Wheeler Field, in the center of Oahu, was the Army's most important base for the aerial defense of the island. One hundred and forty planes from the 14th Fighter Command of the U.S. Army Air Force, most of them P-40B and P-40C fighters, and thirty-nine older P-36 and fourteen P-26 fighters were based at Wheeler. The planes were usually kept in bunkers dispersed around the field, but fear of sabotage had compelled the military to group their planes in the open, in tight formations. This consolidation, put into effect at every air field on Oahu, proved disastrous.

Knocking out Wheeler's planes was a critical part of the Japanese plans, and the attackers expected fierce antiaircraft fire from the field. At 7:55 A.M., as the first wave swept toward its targets, a group of twenty-five Aichi Val dive-bombers from *Zuikaku* came in toward Wheeler from the east, hitting the rows of parked planes, hangars, and other buildings with bombs and then returning to strafe. As gas tanks exploded and planes began to burn, a thick cloud of black smoke rose into the sky.

Antiaircraft fire was minimal. A .50-caliber machine gun on the roof of the firehouse was the only large-caliber weapon immediately available, and it was joined by small arms fire as frustrated soldiers opened up at the low-flying Japanese planes with whatever weapons were at hand. Warrant officer Anthony Albino earned the Silver Star for setting up machine guns on the rear porches of the barracks, and then twice driving through fierce enemy fire to retrieve ammunition. The Vals swept in so low that at least two planes returned to their carriers with telephone wire snagged in their landing gear.

While some men fired at the Japanese, others moved planes out of the way and fought the fires. Their efforts saved several aircraft. Staff Sergeant Charles Fay, from the 72nd Pursuit Squadron, taxied aircraft out of the burning hangars. Wounded twice by machine gun bullets, Fay persisted in his task until the planes were out of danger, earning a Silver Star for his heroism. Wheeler's ground crews also worked feverishly with the pilots to ready several planes that managed to take off from the ravaged field and hit the attacking enemy planes. For their actions, First Lieutenant Malcolm Moore, who helped fight fires and ready his plane before taking off to engage the enemy, Second Lieutenant Philip Rasmussen and First Lieutenant Lewis M. Sanders, who escaped from the holocaust at Wheeler and each shot down an attacking plane, and Second Lieutenant John M. Thacker, another pilot who stayed in the fight until his guns jammed, were awarded the Silver Star.

When the Vals withdrew, a group of Zeros from *Hiryu* hit the field in low-flying strafing runs. The worst damage to Wheeler and its planes had already been done, however. When another group of Zeros from *Hiryu* returned to Wheeler as part of the second attack wave, they added little to the destruction. However, antiaircraft fire hit one of the attacking planes over Wheeler. Zero No. B11-120, flown by Shigenori Saikaijo, was badly damaged. Unable to return to his carrier, Saikaijo crash-landed on Nihau Island. He terrorized the island until one of the residents, Benehakaka Kanahele, twice shot by Saikaijo, killed the Zero pilot in a fierce hand-to-hand battle.

Minutes after the dive-bombers' attack, low-flying Zeros from Hiryu *strafe Wheeler Field.*

Wipeout at Kaneohe

The first bombs to fall on Oahu hit Kaneohe Naval Air Station at 7:48 A.M., seven minutes before Pearl Harbor was attacked. When Fuchida gave the order to deploy at 7:40, a group of dive-bombers and Zeros swung across the island to hit Wheeler Field and Kaneohe. The still unfinished naval air station hosted thirty-six PBY-5 Catalina patrol seaplanes and one utility plane, an OS2U Kingfisher. A contingent of 31 officers, 303 enlisted men, and 96 marines manned Kaneohe.

On the morning of 7 December, three of the lumbering PBYs were on patrol—one of them, piloted by Ensign William Tanner, assisted in spotting and sinking the midget submarine trying to slip past USS *Ward*. Most of the other planes were parked on the seaplane ramp, with four moored in Kaneohe Bay and another four pulled into Hangar No. 1.

The first wave of Japanese planes dove down and

strafed the base, their bullets setting fire to the parked and moored PBYs. The air station's fire fighters rushed to extinguish the burning Catalinas, but the men could do little to save the 34,000-pound, 63-foot-long flying boats. Besides the planes and the men who were killed or injured, the base fire truck and the hangars were also destroyed.

The second wave of attacking planes, including high-altitude bombers and fighters from *Hiryu*, hit Kaneohe again. And when nine Zeros from *Soryu* finished hitting Bellows, they turned to Kaneohe, where their leader, Lieutenant Fusata Iida, was shot down and crashed near officers' housing. Another Zero, trailing smoke, crashed into the bay.

The result of the Japanese attack was, as Rear Admiral Arthur W. Price, Jr., then an aviation metal-smith at Kaneohe, recalled, a "wipeout." Twenty-seven of the PBYs were destroyed, and the other six were badly damaged. Only the three PBYs on patrol when the attack came were left intact.

A number of Kaneohe's men who distinguished themselves were awarded commendations and medals, including Chief Aviation Ordnanceman John William Finn, a Medal of Honor recipient. Finn mounted and worked a .50-caliber machine gun in an exposed position. Despite several wounds, he remained at his post until ordered to seek medical treatment. His wounds dressed, he returned to supervise the rearming of the three PBYs that had just returned from patrol so that they could seek out the withdrawing Japanese forces.

Sailors dash for cover as Kaneohe's PBY-5 Catalinas explode and

bombs spray the tarmac.

Dauntlesses at Ewa Field Explode as Strafing Zeros Attack

Located at Barbers Point west of the harbor entrance, the marine air station at Ewa Mooring Mast Field was the turning point for Fuchida's high-level and torpedo bombers as they began their final attack runs. When the Japanese planes roared overhead toward Pearl at 7:53 A.M., Ewa's officer of the day, Captain Leonard Ashwell, USMC, sounded the alarm, but there was little the marines could do. While they returned fire with pistols and Springfield rifles, Zero fighters from *Kaga* swept in and strafed row after row of planes on the runways. The 20-mm and 7.7-mm bullets, some of them incendiary and explosive rounds, slammed through aluminum fuselages and ruptured fuel tanks, causing planes to explode and sending smoke high into the sky. With several passes at Ewa, the Zeros devastated the field.

Upon returning to *Kaga,* the Zero pilots claimed twenty planes destroyed on the ground with one kill in the air. The Japanese actually destroyed thirty-three of Ewa's forty-nine aircraft. When incoming planes from USS *Enterprise* encountered the Japanese in the air over Ewa, an American SBD-2, piloted by Ensign John Vogt, collided with a Zero, perhaps one of the two from *Kaga* that did not return. Both planes crashed near the intersection of Belt and Ewa Beach roads. Zeros from *Soryu*, flying combat air patrol over Ewa and covering *Kaga*'s planes, also tangled with flyers from *Enterprise* and shot down the SBDs of Ensign John McCarthy and Lieutenant Clarence Dickenson.

As Zeros from Kaga *strafe Ewa, men scramble away from the SBD Dauntlesses that are blossoming into flame and exploding. The Ewa fire truck, shattered by bullets, its tires flat, is nonetheless pressed into service by marines who are trying to put down the flames and salvage what they can.*

Tom Freeman
©1990

The Bombs Fall at Hickam

Hickam Field, at the eastern end of the harbor entrance and immediately south of Battleship Row, was hit hard by the first and second waves. Home of the Hawaiian Air Force, Hickam was commanded by Colonel William F. Farthing and was home to twenty B-17 heavy bombers, thirty-two B-18 medium bombers, and twelve A-20 light bombers. More than half the planes were not airworthy, but a group of B-18s was being prepped for a training flight scheduled to take off at 8:00 A.M. The other planes were grouped together in the middle of the field, ringed by machine guns to protect them from what the Army believed to be the greatest threat, saboteurs.

As the first wave of Japanese aircraft swept in toward Battleship Row, planes from *Shokaku* broke off to hit Hickam. Colonel Farthing and members of his staff, standing in Hickam's control tower waiting for the B-17s to arrive from the mainland, watched horror-struck as a

Japanese plane passed overhead and dropped a torpedo that slammed into a battleship. Then dive-bombing Aichi Vals swooped in, first bombing the hangars and then strafing the field. Men scattered as fuel tanks exploded and shrapnel sprayed the tarmac.

Most of the men who were armed had only .45s or Springfield rifles, but they fired at the strafing planes anyway from beneath vehicles or from the shattered windows of the buildings that ringed the field. A few men managed to fire back with the machine guns, one orderly room clerk mounting a weapon in the turret of a bomber. He kept blazing away as his plane was consumed by flames that had already been licking at the fuselage when he started shooting.

As the nine attacking Vals withdrew, the covering Zeros, commanded by Lieutenant Saburo Shindo from *Akagi,* then strafed the field, making three passes with deadly effect. The Zeros took time out to attack the B-17s

just arriving at the field after a fourteen-hour flight from California. Most of the American bombers managed to land safely, although they were much shot up. The Zeros then withdrew, the first wave of the attack regrouping to return to the carriers.

In the lull that followed, men dragged equipment out of the way of flames and attempted to fight the fires that raged in the hangars and in the tangled masses of aluminum that had once been aircraft. Suddenly, the second wave hit. High-altitude bombers dropped 1,760-pound bombs from nearly 10,000 feet, then a strafing run of Zeros from *Akagi* and *Kaga* hit the airfield again. They left Hickam in shambles.

Two hundred and eighteen soldiers and a number of civilian workers, many of them at Hickam, were killed in the attack. Another 364 Army personnel were wounded. The Army lost 64 planes, and another 128 were damaged, some of them in barely salvageable condition. Hangars, barracks, the officers' club, the base chapel, and several other buildings were left burned, shattered, or destroyed. Left untouched, amazingly enough, was the control tower.

Soldiers at Hickam Field run for cover as strafing planes hit parked B-18 bombers.

"You May Run Into a War during Your Flight": The B-17s Arrive

As the threat of war in the Pacific increased, the United States decided to augment its weak defenses. In answer to Douglas MacArthur's pleas from the Philippines, the U.S. Army Air Force was ordered to fly in squadrons of the Army's new long-range bomber, the B-17. Left unanswered were the pleas of the military commanders in Hawaii. Rather than adding to the defensive force of those islands, the B-17s would merely stop over in Oahu on their long flight to the Philippines.

The 38th and 88th Reconnaissance Squadrons of the USAAF were ordered to fly to Clark Field, stopping to fuel at Hickam Field. Their mission was important, if not critical, and Major General Henry H. "Hap" Arnold flew out to Hamilton Field, north of San Francisco, to address the officers and crews of the eleven bombers that would make the trip. Confident that war would break out by the time they arrived in the Philippines, Arnold told the men of the growing danger of conflict. "War is imminent," he commented. "You may run into a war during your flight."

The B-17s took off from Hamilton Field on the evening of 6 December for the fourteen-hour flight to Oahu. To help guide the planes in, the Hawaiian Air Force asked Honolulu radio station KGMB not to sign off but to broadcast all night long, a standard practice when flights were scheduled to arrive from the mainland.

Each B-17 carried a skeleton crew of just five men—the pilot, copilot, navigator, engineer, and radio operator. The planes were also flying stripped down to save fuel. In answer to an incredulous query from Major Truman H. Landon, commanding officer of the 38th, about why the B-17s' guns and bombsights were to be shipped separately if indeed war was imminent, Arnold had ordered the guns and sights, still packed in

Cosmoline, loaded aboard the planes. There was no ammunition, however, nor men enough to mount and man the guns if the need arose.

The B-17s and the Japanese strike force converged on Oahu at about the same time. The 38th's flight was scheduled to land at 8:00 A.M., but a slight navigation error made the Army bombers ten minutes late. At 8:10 they flew into a holocaust.

As Japanese fighters pounced upon his planes, Landon radioed Hickam to ask if he could land. The tower granted permission, then added, "You have three Japs on your tail." The Zeros poured slugs into Landon's plane, but the rugged bomber withstood the onslaught, as well as hits from ground antiaircraft fire. Dodging and evading the attacking fighters twice, Landon landed at 8:20. The other B-17s also made it down, one with a tail set afire when strafing ignited some magnesium flares inside. Another plane, piloted by Lieutenant Frank Bostrum, managed to make an emergency landing at Kahuku Golf Course with two of its four engines shot out.

Coming in over the tank farm, Major Truman H. Landon is attacked by three Zeros. The Japanese planes pour slugs into Landon's sturdy B-17 as he avoids a hail of irregular and dangerous antiaircraft fire and attempts to land at Hickam Field.

Tom Freeman
© 1990

Brave Frustration: Firing a .45 at the Enemy

The unexpected attack left many of Pearl Harbor's defenders with whatever weapons they had at hand. For the most part, only the Navy ships were able to man large numbers of .30- and .50-caliber machine guns or the heavier 3- and 5-inch antiaircraft guns. On the ground, soldiers, marines, and some sailors at the various air fields had only a few machine guns, Browning Automatic Rifles (BARs), Springfield rifles, and the ubiquitous .45 automatic pistol. One man even hurtled his tools at passing planes in frustration.

A number of men received commendations and medals for quickly setting up and firing machine guns and, in some cases, for downing attacking planes. Staff Sergeant Doyle Kimmey received the Distinguished Service Cross for grabbing a submachine gun and returning the fire of planes strafing Hickam. Staff Sergeant Lowell Klatz and Second Lieutenant Stephen Saltzman, stationed at Wahiawa, earned the Silver Star for leaving the shelter of their post, standing in front of a strafing Japanese plane with automatic rifles, and, with "cool determination and disregard for ... personal safety," shooting it down.

At Kaneohe, an ordnanceman named Sands grabbed a BAR and fired at a passing Zero, which circled and came back, sending bullets slamming into the wall of the building behind him. Piloted by Lieutenant Fusata Iida of *Soryu*, the plane then came back a third time and dived at Sands. The ordnanceman stood his ground a second time and pumped bullets into the cockpit. Iida's plane crashed into a nearby hillside.

Less effective but equally brave were those who used their small arms. A young soldier at Hickam, lying beneath a tractor for cover, fired his .45 whenever a strafing plane passed by, while another man there reportedly fired at the attacking planes with his .45 while riding a bicycle in circles. A man at Kaneohe was also reported to have shot at attacking planes with his .45.

The Japanese pilots witnessed several of these episodes of brave futility, and one man stood out in their memories. He was a lone marine standing by a disabled plane at Ewa, blazing away with his .45 at Lieutenant Yoshio Shiga, who was strafing the field. Though aiming for the marine, Shiga missed, but the "gallant soldier" who had stood his ground had impressed the Japanese pilot. Shiga pulled away, paying his respects to the man, who was probably Private First Class Mel Thompson, stationed at the sentry booth at Ewa's main gate. Like so many others that day, Thompson had responded bravely to the attack that had caught them all off guard and unprepared.

Surrounded by a sea of flames, Private First Class Mel Thomson, USMC, empties his .45 at Lieutenant Yoshio Shiga's Zero.

Fire-Fighting Casualties at Hickam

Next to the bullets and bombs that filled the air, the fires posed the greatest danger and caused the most injuries at Pearl Harbor. Fires raged out of control on many ships, feeding on fuel oil spilled from ruptured bunkers and spreading across the water, and flames engulfed many of the buildings and aircraft ashore.

Fire fighters were for the most part the unsung heroes of Pearl Harbor, dragging hoses, spraying down burning buildings and decks, and hauling engines, guns, and other equipment away from the inferno. These men waged their battle with water and foamite, not bullets. And they fell, not only to smoke and flame, but also to bullets and shrapnel.

Among the fire-fighting heroes were the men of the Hickam Base Fire Department and the crews of six Honolulu Fire Department units that raced to the field to assist them. A bomb hit had demolished Hickam's firehouse, and another bomb had destroyed the fire engine, killing or maiming the crew. Ruptured water mains hindered the men's efforts, but with pumper trucks the fire fighters moved into position.

Fire Chief William L. Benedict, a civilian, was directing his men when he was wounded. He stayed at his post and was hit again, this time more seriously, but he remained until wounded a third time. The chief received the Medal of Merit, one of four awarded civilians for their actions during the attack.

Also recognized for their sacrifice, although belatedly, were three members of the Honolulu Fire Department. Fire fighters were putting out a fierce fire in Hangar No. 21, trying to save the burning Flying Fortress inside, when a dive-bomber scored a direct hit that seriously injured fireman Solomon Naauao. He was unable to continue fighting the fire, but three of his companions, Harry Tuck Lee Pang, Thomas Samuel Macy, and John Carreira, stayed at their posts and were overcome by the spreading inferno. Their families were awarded Purple Heart medals at a special ceremony organized by the National Park Service at the USS *Arizona* Memorial on 7 December 1984.

Corporal Duane W. Shaw, a marine firefighter at Ewa Field, epitomized the attitude of the fire fighters at Hickam, Kaneohe, Wheeler, Ford Island, and Battleship Row. As Zeros set the planes at Ewa ablaze, Shaw and Corporal Carl Hines drove their fire engine across the field to try to save the aircraft. Shaw pressed the pedal to the floor, but strafing bullets shattered the windshield and dimpled the red metal of the truck, then punctured the rear tires. Shaw and Hines sprinted for cover. According to Blake Clark, the first journalist to chronicle the attack, when Shaw was asked by an incredulous officer crouching next to him why he had risked his life, he replied, "Hell, Lieutenant, I saw a fire, and I'm supposed to put 'em out."

A dive-bomber sends a missile hurtling toward the fire fighters of the Honolulu Fire Department who are spraying down a burning Flying Fortress inside Hickam's Hangar 21.

Futility: U.S. Planes Try to Take Off at Bellows Field

The pilots assigned to protect Oahu and the Pacific Fleet were caught, like everyone else, by surprise. While some planes did get off the ground, most were destroyed by strafing and bombs.

At Haleiwa at least six and possibly eight pilots managed to get off the ground during the attack, the most notable being Lieutenants George Welch and Kenneth Taylor. Along with pilots from *Enterprise*, Haleiwa's and Wheeler's airmen were the only ones to dogfight with the Japanese, downing several attacking aircraft. But the Japanese shot down some of *Enterprise*'s planes in the dogfight. They at least had the opportunity to face their foes in the air.

Most pilots did not even have the opportunity to fight back. Three officers were shot down at Bellows Field, on the southeastern end of Oahu, as they attempted to take off. Lieutenant Hans Christiansen of the 44th Pursuit Squadron was climbing into a P-40 at

Bellows when bullets riddled his aircraft and killed him. Two other planes from the 44th Squadron were shot up just after they had lifted off. One, piloted by Lieutenant George Whiteman of the 18th Pursuit Group, had just climbed to a thousand feet when two Zeros came up behind him and poured slugs into his plane, which hit on the beach and burned. The other, piloted by Lieutenant Samuel Bishop, also from the 44th's 18th Pursuit Group, crashed offshore in Kailua Bay, where the wounded Bishop freed himself from the wreckage and swam ashore to Lanikai Beach. Both pilots were awarded the Silver Star for their gallantry, Whiteman posthumously.

The Japanese destroyed at least 162 aircraft that morning, although some sources state that between 169 and 188 American planes were lost. The Navy and Marine Corps suffered the greatest losses—ninety-eight planes (including eleven from *Enterprise*)—while the Army's aircraft losses totaled sixty-four. Additionally, another 159 planes were damaged, the majority of them—128—belonging to the U.S. Army Air Force.

Roaring down the runway, a P-40 lifts in flight as a strafing Zero passes.

Tom Freeman
© 1990

"Against Overwhelming Odds," Welch and Taylor Strike Back

Two of the Army's heroes on 7 December were young lieutenants. George S. Welch and Kenneth M. Taylor, assigned to the 47th Pursuit Squadron, were ending a night-long poker game at the officers' club at Wheeler Field when attacking planes strafed the building. Taylor rushed to his car and picked up Welch, the squadron's assistant operations officer, and the two men drove at breakneck speed to Haleiwa Field, ten miles distant, where the 47th was temporarily based for training exercises. The rest of the squadron was there and the planes were ready to go. Without waiting for orders, Welch and Taylor jumped into their P-40s and took off.

Armed only with .30-caliber ammunition, the two officers flew to Barbers Point and engaged the Japanese before heading to Wheeler, where they landed. As ground crews hastily refueled the planes and loaded .50-caliber ammunition, the second wave of Japanese planes struck. Hastily taking off, bouncing over ammo boxes,

Welch and Taylor climbed into the clouds and then dove into the enemy planes, shooting down two. Under attack again, the two Army pilots moved on to Ewa, where they engaged the Japanese in a dogfight and shot down several planes. When the second wave retreated, Welch circled, looking for more of the enemy, before he and Taylor landed.

Both men received the Distinguished Service Cross. Taylor's citation for his medal summed it up—"initiative, presence of mind, coolness under fire against overwhelming odds ... expert maneuvering ... and determined action. ..."

*An Aichi D-3A1 from the carrier **Akagi** bursts into flame and plummets to the earth as Lieutenants George Welch and Kenneth Taylor dogfight with the planes of the second attack wave in the skies over Barbers Point.*

Tom Freeman
© 1990

"Atarimashita!" *Oklahoma* Is Hit

When Fuchida gave the attack signal, "To, To, To," Lieutenant Shigeharu Murata, leader of the torpedo group, keyed his mike and intoned, "Tsu, Tsu, Tsu," splitting the torpedo pilots up into two attack groups. The veteran battleship *Oklahoma* received much of the torpedo force's attention in the first fifteen minutes of the attack, and the lessons drilled into the Japanese pilots at Kagoshima paid off with deadly effect. Five, perhaps more, of the aerial torpedoes hit against *Oklahoma*'s port side.

Lieutenant Jinochi Goto, squadron commander of the torpedo pilots from *Akagi,* was the first to hit the battleship. Leading a three-plane group toward *Oklahoma,* Goto came in over Hickam Field and then dove toward the water. He leveled out his flight of Nakajima B5N2s at sixty feet over the water and roared toward *Oklahoma,* grasping the release lever. When the ship's hull, 1,500 feet away, all but filled his vision, Goto released the torpedo, which hurtled into the water and struck the battleship with a muffled roar. As he pulled up and passed just over the crow's nest, Goto's observer saw a geyser of water erupt up the ship's side and shouted, "Atarimashita!" ("It hit!").

Looking to his right, Goto saw a torpedo launched by Murata detonate against *West Virginia*. Simultaneously, the two pilots following Goto hit *Oklahoma,* which shuddered under the impact.

On the battleship, general quarters had been sounded. Ensign Herb Rommel grabbed a microphone and made a famous broadcast to the ship's crew over the announcing system: "This is a real Jap air attack and no shit." As his last word came through the annunciators, Goto's torpedo hit. When the next two torpedoes hit home, the ship shuddered and began to roll to port. Knocked off their feet by the blasts, men tumbled to the decks or over the sides into the water. The ship's tor-

pedo blister top disappeared, and the lines securing *Oklahoma* to the battleship *Maryland* began to snap. The order was given to abandon ship, and as word was shouted from man to man, sailors dropped into the oily waters and struck out for *Maryland* or for Ford Island's shores. When *Oklahoma* capsized, its masts bent and broke, its superstructure dug twenty-five feet into the soft harbor mud. With only the bottom sticking above the surface, many of the crew were trapped below decks.

A warhead slams home into the thick skin of USS Oklahoma,

rattling the battleship's rigging and knocking men off their feet.

The Destruction of
USS *Arizona*

After fleet maneuvers off Oahu, *Arizona* entered Pearl Harbor on the morning of Friday, 5 December, and moored on the eastern side of Ford Island at berth F-7. A large number of the men were granted liberty. Work on the ship continued, however. When the repair ship *Vestal* (AR-4) pulled alongside on Saturday, 6 December, the crews of both ships began to make *Arizona* ready for its scheduled repairs. *Vestal* was to fix some of *Arizona*'s equipment so that it wouldn't need to be taken care of during the battleship's upcoming yard period in Bremerton.

Rear Admiral Isaac C. Kidd, who flew his flag aboard *Arizona*, paid a fifteen-minute courtesy call to *Vestal* at 10:00 on Saturday. The forty-eight-year-old captain of the repair ship, Commander Cassin Young, returned the courtesy later in the day when he boarded *Arizona* to discuss the impending work with the battleship's chief engineer.

Work continued into Saturday afternoon. After evening mess the crews turned in, disturbed only by those returning from liberty at midnight.

Meanwhile, off Oahu, the Japanese fleet moved into position and launched the attack. On board *Arizona* and *Vestal* the crews were just beginning the day's activities when the first planes appeared in the sky and the bombs began to fall. *Arizona*'s crew was roused by an explosion that many thought was a torpedo slamming into the battleship's side.

Men raced to their battle stations while machine gun fire from the planes slashed across the decks. *Arizona* was hit several times with bombs. Explosions rocked the ship. The crew rallied to fight the inferno, dragging fire hoses through the thick, choking smoke.

High over the harbor, the ship was silhouetted against the oily waters of the harbor. Petty Officer Noburo Kanai, flying above Battleship Row in a B5N2 Nakajima bomber from the carrier *Soryu,* lined up the stricken battleship in his sights before releasing his bomb. The 1,760-pound missile, a single 16.1-inch shell, plummeted from the sky and struck *Arizona*'s deck near the number two turret. Ripping through steel, the shell penetrated deep into the ship before detonating near the forward magazine.

At that moment, sometime around 8:10, *Arizona* died. The exploding shell set off the powder in the magazine, which erupted in a tremendous blast that rose nearly a thousand feet. The force of the blast burst open the casemates at the bow and bent the deck up and forward, cracking the hull to the keel and nearly tearing the bow free. The decks buckled and gave way, and the number one turret, engulfed in flame, fell into the collapsing hull. The blast swept aft, striking the foremast and superstructure and incinerating every man there, including Captain Franklin Van Valkenburgh and Admiral

Kidd. The foremast tilted forward, and then stopped short of complete collapse. Debris, including parts of bodies, rained down on the harbor, on the decks of other ships, and on Ford Island. A few survivors, their uniforms torn from their bodies, were hurtled through the air into the water.

The fury of the attack continued unabated, and as *Arizona* took additional bomb and possibly torpedo hits, it settled deeper in the water. When the lights went out and smoke and water had spread through the undamaged compartments aft, the senior surviving officer, Lieutenant Commander Samuel Fuqua, directing the now-futile attempts to save *Arizona*, decided to abandon ship. He gave the order at 10:32. Fuqua remained on the quarterdeck while the survivors leaped off the ship or were lowered into nearby boats, and after

one last look, he was the last man to leave.

Three Medals of Honor were awarded for actions aboard *Arizona*—two posthumous awards to Captain Van Valkenburgh and Admiral Kidd, and one to Lieutenant Commander Fuqua.

A roiling mass of flame and destruction pushes out of the ruptured hull of Arizona. *Tons of powder and fuel oil, ignited by a Japanese bomb, tear through the bow, forcing out the casemates and collapsing the decks. Debris and bodies rain across the harbor and Ford Island.*

A Val Is Splashed

Three hundred and fifty aircraft climbed into the skies off Oahu to strike Pearl Harbor. Three hundred and twenty one returned. Lost in the attack were twenty-nine planes and fifty-five airmen, comparatively light losses for the Japanese and much less than the planners had expected. Of these, fifteen were Aichi Vals, nine were Zeros, and five were Nakajima Kates.

Conflicting reports make it difficult to determine just where all the planes went down. More than a hundred vessels' logs comment on splashed or downed planes, many claiming hits. A Navy map drawn in 1942, for example, shows thirty-five crash sites, fourteen of which are on land.

The locations of some planes were well known. Lieutenant Fusata Iida, the leader of Soryu's nine fighters of the second attack wave, was hit by ground fire while strafing Kaneohe and dove into the ground, crashing near the married officers' quarters. Other planes, crashed on land or in the water, were recovered after the attack, and souvenirs from these aircraft are displayed in various museums today. The wing of another downed plane was a prominent souvenir of the marines' First Division until they shipped out for Guadalcanal.

Not all of the planes crashed near Pearl Harbor, some going down near Ewa, shot down by Welch and Taylor, while other planes—damaged, lost, and unable to call for directions to the carriers because of the strict radio silence—probably went down at sea.

Rumors persist of an intact plane in the water of Kaneohe Bay, while another story tells of a crashed Japanese plane on a ridge overlooking Pearl Harbor. Working with the Navy reports, historian Daniel Martinez identified thirteen crash sites in the water that were likely to reveal remains of splashed aircraft. Martinez conjectured, based on the eyewitness accounts, that seven of these were Vals, five were Kates, and the other could be either type of plane. An archaeological survey of the harbor failed to reveal evidence of aircraft at any of the locations: dredging undertaken since 1941 probably eradicated most if not all traces of the crashed planes. Nonetheless, dredging operations in 1990 along Battleship Row near *Oklahoma's* berth recovered a piece of flush-riveted aluminum that may just be a piece of one of the elusive Japanese aircraft.

Hit by antiaircraft fire, its engine flaming and its crew dead, an

Aichi Val plummets toward the water.

Cassin (DD-372) and *Downes* (DD-375) Erupt in Dry Dock

Inside Dry Dock No. 1, the battleship *Pennsylvania* (BB-38), flagship of the Pacific Fleet, and the destroyers *Cassin* (DD-372) and *Downes* (DD-375) sat out the first attack wave, high and dry on blocks. The two destroyers, side by side, were ahead of the battleship in the sunken concrete berth, close to *Pennsylvania*'s bow, which loomed over the two tin cans' fantails.

As the violence of the first attack wave swept past them, the men of the three ships raced to join in the defense of the fleet. *Pennsylvania*'s .50-caliber guns opened up immediately, while men raced to fit the belts and breech blocks to the .50-caliber machine guns and 5-inch guns on the destroyers. Within forty-five minutes the guns were ready, and the three ships in the dry dock added to the now-intensifying antiaircraft fire climbing into the sky.

The second wave of attacking planes, now over Pearl, returned the fire. The dive-bombers split into two groups, one to attack *Nevada*, then making a run for the sea, the other to strike the ships in dry dock, including the destroyer *Shaw*. Aichi Val dive-bombers attacked the hitherto neglected ships in Dry Dock No. 1. At 9:07 a 250-kilogram bomb hit *Pennsylvania*, tearing into the starboard side at frame 83, while a bomb hit *Downes'* superstructure and demolished the bridge.

Another 250-kilogram bomb slammed into the fantail of *Cassin*. It tore through the destroyer, passed through the bottom at frame 140, and struck the floor of the dry dock, starting a fire. The crews fought the encroaching flames from the decks of the ships, but the fire advanced. Then more bombs hit both sides of the dry dock, cutting off electrical power and water to the dock, and a second bomb hit *Cassin* at frame 60 and tore open the fuel bunkers of both destroyers.

Yard worker Ed Sheehan, nearby, watched as "a crane moving alongside the dry dock stopped" when the power was cut off. Then "flames leaped out of the big sunken basin and smoke whorled up" when the oil

spilling from the ruptured hulls ignited. Men who had previously raced to fire back at the Japanese planes now fought the flames that spread throughout the dry dock.

The order was given to flood the dry dock, and at 9:20 the water started pouring in, coated with thick oil that fouled the ships and clung to every surface. Flames engulfed the two destroyers, and the order was passed to abandon ship.

As the water rose it floated *Cassin*'s stern and pivoted the destroyer around. It toppled against *Downes*. Yard workers, sailors, and marines on the sidelines poured water on the blazing hulks, devoting much of their attention to the ship's depth-charge racks and torpedoes. The flames gained on them, however, despite the arrival of a pumper truck from the Base Fire Department, and at 9:30 the magazines and torpedoes "cooked off" aboard *Downes*.

Yard Photographer Tai Sing Loo, helping fight the fire, said that suddenly a "terrific explosion came from the destroyer." A "few people were hurt, some fell down" as chunks of steel ripped through the dock, hitting *Pennsylvania*'s bow. A half-ton piece of wreckage from the torpedo launchers landed on the battleship's forecastle. Regaining their feet, the fire fighters returned to their task with a vengeance, and at 10:45 the flames were extinguished, leaving charred wreckage floating in the flooded dry dock, the destroyers locked in a mangled embrace, and the bow of *Pennsylvania* scorched and pocked.

The battleship's damage was repaired quickly, but practicality meant salvaging only the machinery of the two destroyers, not the surviving portions of the hulls. The machinery was shipped to the mainland, where *Cassin* and *Downes* were reborn in new hulls at Mare Island, returning to the war in November 1943 and February 1944, respectively.

Burning fuel fills Dry Dock No. 1 while yard workers and the crew of Pennsylvania *spray down the blazing hulks of* Cassin *and* Downes.

USS *Nevada* (BB-36) Makes a Gallant Run for the Sea

When the first wave of planes struck at 7:55, USS *Nevada* (BB-36), moored near *Arizona,* had partial steam up. At 8:03 the battleship took its first hit: a torpedo slammed into the hull near frame 41, tearing a 48 by 25–foot hole in the side. Quick-thinking officers counter flooded and corrected the ship's list, and antiaircraft guns opened up on the attacking planes.

The commanding officer, Captain F. W. Scanland, was not aboard, and the senior officer on the ship was Lieutenant Commander J. F. Thomas, USNR. Thomas and another junior officer conned the damaged *Nevada* away from Battleship Row at 8:45, as burning oil from the sunken and blazing hulk of *Arizona* swept toward them and the second wave of Japanese planes struck Pearl Harbor. The officers hoped to escape the trap and run for the open sea through the narrow harbor entrance.

In part for his valorous actions in casting off the ship

from the mooring quays and then swimming back to *Nevada*, Chief Warrant Officer (Boatswain) Edwin Joseph Hill, killed as the ship ran for the sea, was awarded a posthumous Medal of Honor. Machinist Donald K. Ross, twice dragged unconscious from his post but returning to his dangerous station each time, received *Nevada*'s second Medal of Honor. Additionally, fourteen members of the crew received the Navy Cross for their heroic actions.

As *Nevada* passed Battleship Row, pilots from the carrier *Kaga* seized the chance to sink the ship in the channel and block the harbor entrance. Dive-bombers swooped in, hitting *Nevada* with five 250-kilogram bombs that holed the forward decks and superstructure. At 9:07, as the battleship passed 1010 Dock, dive-bombers massed another attack. One bomb hit the forecastle, which blossomed into flame, while strafing Zeros swooped in over Ford Island.

At the dock Rear Admiral William Rea Furlong, aboard his damaged and sinking flagship *Oglala*, saw *Nevada* shudder under the impact of the bombs and ordered the yard tug *Hoga*, then assisting him, to rush to the aid of the battleship. With YT-130, *Hoga* pulled the burning *Nevada* off Hospital Point, where the officers had beached the sinking ship. The tugs pulled *Nevada* to Waipio Point, and the battleship was allowed to settle into the mud, its massive guns pointing to sea. Tied to the port bow, *Hoga*'s crew poured water on the burning forecastle for over an hour before leaving *Nevada*.

Swooping over Ford Island, two Zeros strafe the battleship Nevada *as the mortally wounded battleship passes 1010 Dock on its run for the sea. A bomb hit on the forecastle has already blazed into flame.*

Neosho (AO-23) Averts a Holocaust

One of the most fortunate aspects of Pearl Harbor was the Japanese failure to attack the tank farm with its millions of gallons of fuel oil for the Pacific Fleet. Another lucky break was the escape of the tanker *Neosho* (AO-23). Laden with volatile aviation gasoline, the tanker was moored in an exposed position in the middle of the attack. As Lawson Ramage, watching from across the harbor, later commented, "If they had blown up the *Neosho*, that would have been the end of everything… ." *Neosho*'s escape was in part luck but mostly the result of skillful thinking and quick handling on the part of its officers and crew.

Neosho had arrived from San Pedro, California, at 6:53 on the morning of 6 December. Saturday was spent discharging fuel at Hickam Field, a task that was finished at 7:10 P.M., at which time *Neosho* moved to Ford Island. The tanker moored at Berth F4 at 9:40 and started pumping gasoline at 10:59. The crew worked through the night and finished fueling at Ford at 7:50 on the morning of the 7th. A few minutes later, while the pumps were still working at back suction to clear the fueling lines, the first wave of Japanese aircraft hit.

The Japanese torpedo planes ignored *Neosho*, managing nonetheless to sink *Oklahoma* and *California*, the battleships moored at either end of the tanker. As explosions rocked the harbor, Commander John S. Phillips, *Neosho*'s commanding officer, his crew, and personnel from Ford Island sprang into action to clear the still-laden tanker. They knew that one hit on *Neosho* would turn Battleship Row, already a blazing inferno, into a holocaust. General quarters was sounded on the tanker at 8:00, and ten minutes later its antiaircraft batteries opened fire.

On the gasoline dock, the fuel officer, Ensign D. Arnold Singleton, Chief Machinist's Mate Alfred Hansen, and Aviation Machinist's Mate Second Class Albert Thatcher worked to disconnect the fuel lines. Strafing planes sprayed the dock with lead, wounding Hansen and Thatcher. Singleton turned on the sprinklers that surrounded Ford Island's fuel tanks to avert the danger of fire if the tanks were hit. Other men on the dock helped cut *Neosho*'s mooring lines free.

Phillips backed his ship out of Battleship Row without waiting for tugs because burning oil from the blazing battleships was drifting toward the tanker. Turning at an awkward angle to avoid hitting the capsized *Oklahoma*, *Neosho* ran backwards across the channel toward the Merry Point fuel piers, Japanese planes roaring overhead. The tanker ended its short sortie without harm but would not be so lucky in its confrontation with the Japanese at the Battle of the Coral Sea a few months later.

Backing away from Ford Island, Neosho *avoids Japanese planes.*

A burning Val arches away from the tanker and passes the bow of

California.

Tom Freeman
© 1990

St. Louis (CL-49) Clears the Harbor

The only large ship to clear the carnage of Pearl Harbor during the attack was the light cruiser *St. Louis* (CL-49). Moored in Southeast Loch next to the cruiser *Honolulu*, *St. Louis*'s stern faced the slot that Japanese torpedo bombers raced down as they launched their missiles against Battleship Row. *St. Louis*'s guns opened up on the Kates immediately, splashing one before the order to commence firing was given. Captain George A. Rood later recalled with pride that "our battery people knew what was up, knew what to do and did it"; they took "the initiative and opened fire with everything that would bear." *St. Louis*'s gunners were credited with three enemy planes.

The cruiser was under repair, with two boilers down, a large hole cut in the side, and wooden scaffolding on deck. As the guns hammered at the attacking planes strafing the ship, the crew welded the plates shut and tore the scaffolding down and threw it over the side. In the engine room, the "black gang" stoked the boilers and raised partial steam by 9:30. A bomb hit *Honolulu* at 9:31, and the concussion jolted *St. Louis,* knocking a few men off their feet as the cruiser slowly backed out of its berth and turned, stern first, toward Battleship Row.

Captain Rood had decided to run for the sea, and he ordered full emergency speed to take the cruiser past the burning hulks on the Row. *St. Louis* passed through the flames spreading across the oil slick from *Oklahoma*'s ruptured bunkers and dashed forward at 22 knots, ramming through and severing a mooring cable that stretched across the water in its way.

At the helm was a teenage seaman, Daniel Patrick O'Conner, who was standing his first watch as a special-sea-detail helmsman. Watching only the compass and the wheel indicator, O'Conner spun the helm and executed the ordered turns with quick precision, earning a "well done" from the captain.

To Boatswain's Mate Howard French, watching from Ford Island as *St. Louis* swept past, the cruiser with its crew at battle stations was a thrilling sight: "no one seemed to give a damn. ... That skipper was really moving and it looked as though no one but God himself was going to stop him." Passing the stricken *California,* *St. Louis* dashed through the Outer Channel, picking up speed when Rood noticed two torpedoes streaking across the water toward him. As the cruiser reached 25 knots and turned, the torpedoes hit submerged coral heads or a spit near the ship, detonating with a roar.

St. Louis's officers spotted the conning tower of a midget submarine, and the cruiser fired at the target, which was hit or submerged. The ship then ran toward Waikiki, avoiding another torpedo track as it made its way to the open sea. There the cruiser joined a few other ships to search unsuccessfully for the Japanese fleet.

St. Louis exits Pearl Harbor as flames and smoke from the burning Arizona *fill the sky.*

Tom Freeman
©1999

"We Four Ensigns" of USS *Aylwin* (DD-355)

The destroyer *Aylwin* (DD-355) was moored in a nest with the other three destroyers—*Farragut* (DD-348), *Dale* (DD-353), and *Monaghan* (DD-354)—of Destroyer Division 2 on the morning of 7 December. When Japanese planes roared overhead, the four ships sprang into action, opening up with their 5-inch and .50-caliber guns.

At 8:10, with smoke drifting across the water from the burning *Arizona*, the signal flags of *California* ordered all ships to sortie. *Monaghan*, the duty destroyer, was the first to raise steam.

Aylwin's senior officers were ashore, and the only officers left on the ship were four ensigns with a combined sea experience of little more than a year. The senior ensign, Sidney Caplan, had seven months' experience. Caplan assumed command, while Ensign Hugo C. Anderson acted as executive officer, Ensign William K. Reordan served as gunnery officer, and Ensign Burdick H. Brittin was the torpedo officer. With only "we four ensigns," as Brittin called them, in command, *Aylwin* sortied.

During the initial minutes of the attack, *Aylwin*'s guns blazed at attacking planes that were concentrating on USS *Curtiss*. Bombs fell close to the destroyers, severing *Aylwin*'s bow mooring. A near miss hit near the stern, shoving the fantail against an anchor buoy, "and we could feel the ship vibrate, signifying that we had damaged one of our screws."

Just after 8:37 the destroyers started moving, *Monaghan* in the lead, to begin their dash down the channel. Brittin's reaction is revealing: "From then until we had cleared … I was nearer to death and yet lived more than any other person I have ever spoken to. … The channel ahead of us was a mass of bomb explosions from high flying bombs, and at the time all the officers aboard were certain we would never get through." Working on the deck in his dress whites and wearing a steel helmet, Brittin helped push all flammable materials over the side—barrels of lube oil, the whaleboat, and even the ship's mahogany accommodation ladder. Strafing planes continued to pass overhead.

Commodore Ralph S. Riggs of DesDiv 2 and Captain Robert H. Rodgers of *Aylwin* chased down their destroyer outside the harbor in a boat, but the junior officers were under orders not to stop for fear of enemy submarines, so they had to leave the senior officers behind, steaming away to join the other ships that had made a successful escape. "We considered it foolhardy to stop despite the fact that the captain's small boat tried to close us numerous times. The opportunity is rare indeed for an ensign to refuse his captain's request to come aboard, and further, to sail off with his ship. We did just that."

After a day and a night of cruising and searching for the enemy, *Aylwin* returned to port. "We were silent as we went in, for fires still burned and hangars and planes and homes were mere rubble."

Hailing Aylwin, *the destroyer's captain and admiral futilely try to board the ship after its dash from the devastation of Pearl Harbor.*

Burning and Falling Out of Control, a Kate Dives into the Seaplane Tender *Curtiss* (AV-4)

At 8:36 the crew of the seaplane tender *Curtiss,* which was moored off Pearl City in Middle Loch the morning of 7 December, sighted a Japanese midget submarine in the harbor and opened fire on it. At the same time, the sub fired a torpedo at the seaplane tender. The torpedo missed, but *Curtiss*'s shots damaged the submarine and brought it to the surface, where it was finished off by *Monaghan*.

At 8:53, when the second wave of planes roared over Pearl Harbor, the Japanese pilots concentrated much of their attention on the Middle and East Lochs. *Curtiss* opened fire immediately and attracted the attention of the dive-bombers, who zeroed in on the seaplane tender. The falling bombs missed the ship, but a Japanese plane that was shot down hit *Curtiss,* causing devastating damage.

The plane, a Nakajima B5N2 Kate torpedo bomber from *Akagi,* was piloted by Lieutenant Mimori Suzuki.

Aylwin, Blue, Tangier, Patterson, and *Detroit* all claimed they fired the fatal shots. Ted Hechler, Jr., aboard *Phoenix,* saw the Kate roar by as Suzuki throttled down and dropped his torpedo. "He banked to the left as he got opposite us, as if to turn away. I could see .50-caliber tracer slugs going right out to the plane and passing through the fuselage at the wing joint. Suddenly, flames shot out from underneath, and he continued his turn and bank to the left until he had rolled over onto his back. A great cheer went up from our crew… ." The cheers turned to groans when Suzuki's plane rammed into *Curtiss* at 9:05.

The Kate hit the No. 1 crane and exploded in a ball of fire that shot across the boat deck. Just seven minutes later another plane dropped a bomb that hit in the same area, spreading destruction and fire through the hangar. *Curtiss* listed to starboard. The Japanese intensified their attack on the seaplane tender, and near misses continued to strike alongside the ship. *Curtiss* and nearby ships were hard pressed to shoot down the attacking planes.

The attack abated a half hour later, leaving *Curtiss* out of commission. Three near misses had badly damaged the hull, while the bomb that hit the ship had joined Suzuki's plane to damage three deck levels.

Curtiss was repaired at Pearl Harbor, entering dry dock on 19 December. After leaving dry dock on the 27th, the ship was set aside so that other more needed vessels could be repaired, and it did not return for final repairs until late April of the following year. *Curtiss* was not restored to action until 28 May 1942.

Flames blossom from the fuselage of Lieutenant Mimori Suzuki's Nakajima Kate torpedo bomber. Hit by gunfire from one or perhaps several nearby ships and dead at the controls, Suzuki rides his plane down toward Curtiss. *Within seconds, he will crash into the ship and explode into a ball of flame.*

TOM FREEMAN
©1990

Monaghan (DD-354) Rams and Sinks a Midget

The destroyer *Monaghan* (DD-354) entered Pearl Harbor on the morning of Saturday, 6 December, and moored at Berth X-14 in East Loch along with the other vessels of Destroyer Division Two—*Dale, Aylwin,* and *Farragut*. The commanding officer of *Monaghan* was hard-driving Commander William P. Burford. That afternoon, Burford prepared his crew with fire, collision, and fire and rescue drills because *Monaghan* was the ready-duty destroyer. If called to action, the destroyer would be able to put to sea within an hour.

The call came the next morning. The report of *Ward's* skipper, William Outerbridge, that his ship had sunk a submarine operating in the defensive zone reached the headquarters of the 14th Naval District at 7:10. On his own initiative the officer in charge contacted *Monaghan* and ordered it to sea, where it would contact *Ward*. As the destroyer was making its final preparations to steam, the first wave of the attacking Japanese planes struck Pearl Harbor.

It was at this moment, according to the Japanese plan, that the midget submarines would rise from the harbor and press forward with their attack. At 8:30 the minesweeper *Zane* (DMS-14) spotted a midget submarine two hundred yards aft of *Medusa* (AR-1) at Berth K-23. *Zane*'s report was quickly noted, and at 8:32 Commander-in-Chief Pacific Fleet sent out an alert: "Japanese submarine in harbor."

Monaghan was already underway and was passing Pearl City when *Curtiss* reported its encounter with a midget submarine at 8:36. At 8:39, just as Commander Burford was dismissing the account with the admonition that *Curtiss* was "crazy," his signalman spotted the surfacing submarine off the starboard bow, its bow pointed at the oncoming destroyer. Burford ordered flank speed and raced toward the submarine, intent on ramming it.

Curtiss fired on the tiny craft with 5-inch and .50-caliber shells, and the tender *Tangier* did also until

Monaghan blocked the target. A hit from *Curtiss*'s 5-inch guns tore through the midget's conning tower, decapitating the sub commander and pinning his body in the mangled steel. Then *Monaghan* hit the foundering midget with a glancing blow, starboard side to port side, "shoving the submarine out of sight," according to the log of the nearby *Medusa*.

As the submarine sank, its second torpedo fired, passed under *Monaghan*, and hit the banks of Ford Island, where it exploded. The crew of the destroyer rolled two depth charges off the stern as the ship passed over its victim, and the detonations bodily lifted *Monaghan*'s stern out of the water while pulverizing the midget's hull. *Monaghan* continued forward, ramming a burning dredge before backing off, grounding temporarily, and proceeding to sea.

When the midget submarine was raised a few days later, the uniform insignia of the dead commander was cut off. Captured submariner Sakamaki, whose *HA-19* had failed to penetrate the harbor and had washed ashore the following day, was shown the insignia. In his memoirs, Sakamaki claimed it was that of Lieutenant Naoji Iwasa, leader of the midget submarine attack force, who had launched from *I-22*. The damaged submarine was dumped into a landfill at the submarine base in early 1942 when a new quay wall was built and forgotten until 1952, when work in the area uncovered the buried hulk. The midget was pushed deeper into the fill and reburied with the remains of Lieutenant Iwasa and his fellow crew member, Petty Officer First Class Naokichi Sasaki, still aboard.

USS Monaghan *surges ahead and rams into a surfaced Japanese midget submarine, driving into the steel-hulled craft with deadly force to send it to the depths of Pearl Harbor.*

Hoga (YT-146) Tackles *Arizona's* Fires

The yard tug *Hoga* (YT-146) was moored with other yard service craft at 1010 Dock on the morning of 7 December. Ten of the tug's eleven crewmen were aboard—the cook was ashore. Assistant Tugmaster Robert Brown, asleep in the pilothouse, was awakened by the dropping bombs. "I raised up and looked out and all hell was breaking loose." Chief Boatswain's Mate Joseph McManus, the Tugmaster, also heard the explosions while he was shaving in his cabin. "I looked out the porthole … and the first sight I saw was *Oklahoma* which had quite a list. The Chief Engineer was standing on the dock and I heard him say, 'My God! This is war!'" McManus ordered the tug's powerful diesel-electric engines fired up as the officer in charge of the yard craft ran to the dock to yell his orders "to get underway and assist wherever we could." These were the only orders *Hoga* received.

Racing toward Battleship Row, already wreathed in

flame and blanketed in smoke, the tug hove to and plucked two men from the water before continuing to the blazing wreck of *Arizona*. Throwing lines to *Vestal*, *Hoga* pulled the repair ship away from the battleship at 8:30. Running back to 1010 Dock, the tug was hailed by Rear Admiral William Rea Furlong from his flagship *Oglala* and asked to pull the sinking minelayer out of the field of fire for the cruiser *Helena*. Afterward, Furlong ordered *Hoga* back into the channel to assist the now stranded and burning *Nevada*. With YT-130, *Hoga* pulled the battleship free of the mud at Hospital Point. The tug then played its monitors onto *Nevada*'s burning forecastle. From *Nevada*, the tug headed down Battleship Row, battling blazes on *Maryland, Tennessee,* and finally *Arizona*.

Pushing up against the burning hulk and cutting through the flames on the oil-stained waters, *Hoga* threw streams of water at the battleship for nearly seventy-two hours. Assistant Tugmaster Brown, from his vantage point on *Hoga*'s deck, saw a sobering sight: "dead bodies … we could see them up on the mainmast" and scattered on the decks. "We didn't recover any bodies," however, because "we had more important work to do," stated Brown.

On Tuesday, 9 December, the fires were extinguished, and *Hoga* was released to recover bodies and help patrol the harbor for Japanese midget submarines believed to be lurking in the shallows.

For the actions of his ship and crew, McManus was commended for distinguished service and efficient action in assisting *Nevada* and helping extinguish the inferno on Battleship Row "in a most efficient manner" with "commendable disregard of personal danger."

Smoke-streaked and exhausted, the crew of the yard tug Hoga *sprays down the inferno that rages aboard* Arizona. *Thick smoke and burning fuel oil drift across the tug as the pilothouse monitor steadily discharges into the flames.*

"To Live and Fight Another Day": Rescuing Men from USS *Oklahoma*

When torpedoes slammed into the side of *Oklahoma,* the decks writhed from the impact of the explosions. Below decks, sailors watched in horror as the ship slowly began to list. Seaman Stephen Young, in the powder-handling room of his turret, saw "gear of all descriptions … tumble about" as sailors scrambled for the emergency escape tube. "But it was useless; they got stuck before they could make it out," trying to climb down into the waters pouring in from the now-submerged decks of the capsizing ship. Shells in the handling room broke loose, caroming off the bulkheads and sliding across the tilted decks to smash into men who could not get out of the way. Men clung to ladders, powder hoists, and fittings as the deck slipped from beneath their feet, leaving them dangling above the debris-, body-, and water-filled compartments.

Clinging with all his remaining strength, Stephen Young felt the battleship give one more lurch. "As she rolled over, I was pitched into a mass of dead and dying and, then, with them, buffeted and tossed about. Then the dark waters closed over me as the ship came to rest upside down on the bottom of the harbor." Fighting to the surface of the oily waters, Young and several of his shipmates then made their way into a less-flooded compartment.

With battle lanterns, the men searched for ways to escape, and most found all avenues of egress blocked. After holding his breath and transiting a flooded passageway, Young found a porthole with a dead body wedged tightly in it. Out of a group of thirty men, Young's party dwindled to less than twenty as sailors slowly slipped off to look for a way out. Others lay quietly in the darkness, shivering with cold, lungs choked with the thick fuel oil that coated the compartments.

The water rose inch by inch, forcing Young and his fellow survivors to retreat to the drier lucky bag compartment, where they lay on mattresses and peacoats to await death. Gradually, the air turned foul. Through the bulkhead they heard the voices of other men, but in time talking again gave way to silence, and for some to prayer. Imprisoned in a "dark iron cell," Stephen Young was angered by his impending death.

Meanwhile, on the surface, where *Oklahoma*'s hull rose above the water, screws and bilge keels and red bottom paint glinting in the sun, sailors and yard workers labored to free the men who were shouting and rapping on the steel shell with wrenches. On the overturned *Utah*, workers also raced to cut the hull to free the men trapped inside. Only one man from *Utah*, fireman John B. Vaessen, was saved.

Acetylene torches were used to cut into the bottom of *Oklahoma*, but the fumes were deadly, or the little air remaining was burned away, and the men inside suffocated. In other cases, the air inside the ship, under pressure, was released when the hull was cut, and the water completely flooded the compartment and drowned the trapped men before they could be freed. Pneumatic drills and chisels were then used to slowly hack at the thick steel plates, and it was in this fashion, on the morning of 8 December, that Stephen Young and a number of other men were finally rescued.

Communicating with the workers above them by tapping out messages in Morse code against the bulkhead, the sailors in the darkness watched as a hole was drilled through the hull into their compartment. As the air hissed out, the water shot in. The hatch into the next compartment was dogged shut, "but water continued to spray in the sides." Now the rescue workers raced to chisel into the plate steel, and their air hammers clanged against the hull. When the water was waist high, the plate was bent enough to pass the oil-slicked sailors out, and they moved from compartment to compartment until they were hauled from holes cut in the ship's bottom.

The first men rescued from *Oklahoma* reached air and light once more at 8:00 A.M. on 8 December; Young and some of his mates were freed at 9:00 A.M., and through the rest of the morning and early afternoon another twenty-four sailors were freed. The last man removed alive from the hulk of the battleship was found at 2:30 A.M. on 9 December. A watch remained on the overturned hull until 11 December, but no other signs of life were heard from *Oklahoma*. Thirty-two men were rescued from their dark, half-flooded tomb; more than four hundred bodies were recovered later when the ship was raised.

Even grimmer yet was the discovery aboard *West Virginia* when it was raised. Sixty-seven bodies were recovered, including those of three men in a storeroom. Trapped in an unflooded compartment in the sunken hulk, the three had lived in the darkness until their air gave out on 23 December, nearly three weeks after the attack.

Transfigured by the light coming in through the holes that yard workers are cutting in the plates of the hull, sailors trapped in the capsized, water- and oil-filled hull of USS Oklahoma *taste fresh air and freedom after twenty-five hours in darkness.*

The Last Detail: Striking *Arizona's* Colors

*A*rizona's leaking oil bunkers fueled an inferno that blazed away on the battleship's destroyed foredeck and superstructure for three days. Aft of the mainmast, the flames scarcely touched the ship, which only a couple of hours after the attack was slowly settling into the soft mud of the harbor.

Arizona's survivors abandoned ship at 10:32 A.M. The senior surviving officer, Lieutenant Commander Sam Fuqua, was the last man to leave. Except for the men of the fire-fighting tug *Hoga* (YT-146), who briefly boarded the battleship while they were putting out the fires, the last to board *Arizona* on 7 December were Lieutenant Kleber S. Masterson and Ensign Leon Grabowsky.

Ashore on leave during the attack, Masterson drove to Pearl Harbor, where he assisted with first aid and helped muster the ship's survivors. "There weren't many," Masterson later said. "Out of eighty-four men in my fire control division, I think there were five survivors."

Temporarily assigned to *Maryland*, Masterson enlisted the services of Grabowsky, another survivor from *Arizona*, to go back aboard their ship and retrieve the tattered, oil-stained flag left flying from the fantail. "It was the big Sunday ensign flying from the stern, and it was dragging in the water and getting all messed up with oil." Motoring over in a launch, the two men stepped up onto the quarterdeck, now littered with debris. "We heard no noises, because there were, of course, no survivors under that little bit of deck we could walk on." As the sun set, Grabowsky lowered the ensign while Masterson gathered the oily flag into his arms. With darkness falling to end the day of infamy, the two men returned to *Maryland* and handed the flag over to the officer of the deck. They never saw it again. Masterson was informed that the flag had been burned.

Arizona continued to settle, and within a few days the waters of Pearl Harbor had forever closed over the fantail.

Smoke climbs into the sky from the burning, shattered hulk of USS Arizona *as the sun sets over Pearl Harbor. Standing on the fantail, Lieutenant Kleber Masterson and Ensign Leon Grabowsky lower the colors from the battleship's stern.*

Epilogue: Fifty Years Later

In the aftermath of the attack on Pearl Harbor the U.S. Navy commenced repair and salvage work and succeeded in raising all of the sunken vessels with the exception of *Arizona* and *Utah*. Of the vessels raised, all were salvaged and returned to duty save *Oklahoma*, which sat at Pearl Harbor through the war, was sold for scrap, and sank while under tow in 1947. Of the ninety-seven U.S. ships at Pearl Harbor and the twenty-eight Japanese vessels assembled for the "Hawaii Operation" on that fatal day, only a handful survived sinking or scrapping. The former U.S. Coast Guard cutter *Taney* is now a museum ship in Baltimore, Maryland. The only known U.S. Navy ship left afloat is the former *Hoga* (YT-146), now the fireboat *City of Oakland* in its namesake port. Two of the Japanese midget submarines survive. One of them, Ensign Sakamaki's *HA-19*, was captured at Bellows on 8 December and exhibited in a nationwide War Bond drive before ending up at Key West. Now temporarily displayed at the Nimitz Museum in Fredericksburg, Texas, the midget will return to Pearl Harbor for display in 1993. Another midget, raised in 1960 from the waters off Pearl, was returned to Japan and is displayed at Eta Jima.

The most significant of all these vessels rests where it was sunk on 7 December. USS *Arizona* and the *Arizona* Memorial have become a major shrine and point of remembrance not only for the lost battleship but for the entire attack. Millions of people now visit *Arizona* annually and quietly file through its memorial, toss flower wreaths and leis into the water, and look at the visible pieces of the rusting hulk that rise above the oil-stained water.

While *Arizona* was investigated and surveyed soon after the attack, it was decided only to remove its topsides, which stuck above the water, and to salvage the armament because wartime priorities precluded further work. When the limited salvage work was finished, the vessel was left as a memorial to its crew. In 1942 a new battleship berth was constructed on *Arizona*'s hulk. The steel and concrete quays were also used as landings by Navy crews who came to raise and lower the United States flag flying from a pole welded to the severed stub of the battleship's mainmast, and for memorial services.

The need for a larger, more-fitting memorial was realized in 1958, and in 1961 appropriations for the current structure were approved. The memorial structure was completed in 1962 at a cost of $500,000. By the late 1970s visitation at the memorial had increased tremendously. When 1980 legislation authorized the National Park Service (NPS) to operate the new USS *Arizona* Memorial Visitor Center, the U.S. Navy and the NPS worked cooperatively to preserve and interpret the story of *Arizona*, *Utah*, the Pearl Harbor attack, and the Pacific forces' wartime actions through the Battle of

Midway in 1942. The NPS now manages the modern visitor center, which houses major exhibits, including attack artifacts and models and graphics of the battleship as it was and as it sits now beneath the arched memorial's gleaming white walls.

The partnership between the U.S. Navy and the NPS has also provided a much more detailed view of the aftermath of the Pearl Harbor attack, and the NPS has studied this battle by investigating the underwater remains of the battlefield. The NPS has the only federal team of underwater archaeologists, the Submerged Cultural Resources Unit. Initially asked to help understand just what was left of *Arizona*, the unit's chief, Daniel Lenihan, worked with archaeologists Larry Murphy and Larry Nordby and scientific illustrator Jerry Livingston to capture *Arizona* and *Utah* on video, slide film, and mylar. The resulting images provide a unique view of the events of fifty years ago. The

drawings and photographs, and a model of the sunken hulk done by Robert F. Sumrall, now present a more graphic view of *Arizona* to the visiting public.

Archaeology, as the means of studying human behavior through its physical or material manifestations, is valid even when examining recent events, as the NPS's work at Pearl Harbor has demonstrated. There is a history of Pearl Harbor that is in part myth and in part folklore founded on imperfect memory and recollection. The best example is the story that a bomb dropping down the ship's stack had destroyed *Arizona*. Lenihan and Murphy found no archaeological evidence to support this hypothesis—in fact, they found evidence contrary to it, namely, that the stack gratings were intact.

The historical record of the attack was a complete failure in one instance. Based on the extensive surviving documentation of the salvage of the battleship, the archaeologists expected that no guns remained on the ship. Yet the first dive showed that the No. 1 turret, with its three 14-inch guns, is still mounted.

One of the major questions for the survey was the extent of damage done by Japanese torpedoes. Survivors claim that *Arizona* was hit by at least two torpedoes, one of which passed beneath the repair ship *Vestal*, which was moored to the battleship. *Arizona* was also hit by aerial bombs, one of which is generally credited by historical accounts as the agent of the battleship's destruction. Navy divers assessing the battle damage in 1942 found evidence that a 1,760-pound projectile had hit near *Arizona*'s No. 2 turret, penetrated several decks, and detonated near the forward magazines, touching off nearly a million pounds of powder. This explosion demolished the forward sections of the ship, pushed out the casemates and hull above the waterline at the bow, lifted decks vertically, and collapsed the No. 1 turret and its barbette by some twenty-eight feet. No discussion of torpedo damage was recorded, and later archaeological investigation has been fruitless because the ship had sunk into the harbor mud, and silt had built up to cover the underwater hull areas. If there was any torpedo damage, it was effectively hidden.

Archaeological evidence for the aerial-bomb theory recently surfaced when the Aberdeen Proving Ground Museum in Maryland turned up the base plate from what has been identified as a 16.1-inch Japanese naval shell recovered from the forward area of *Arizona*. Yet there is neither positive nor negative archaeological evidence at this time to use to assess the question, so thus far archaeology cannot conclusively determine what sank *Arizona*. There remains the Navy's conjecture, which the NPS has found no evidence to refute based on its research to date. Excavating silt and mud away from the ship to investigate its port side, where the torpedoes would have hit, might resolve the question.

More instructive than the battle damage was what was done to *Arizona* after the battle. The Pearl Harbor salvage was one of the most comprehensive and costly maritime salvage operations of modern times. The first priority was the recovery of antiaircraft guns and their gun directors, a logical first order of business for a fleet subjected to devastating aerial assaults. Next in priority were other armament, followed by ammunition and then complete ships. Those ships that had been lightly damaged were repaired and rushed into service, while more difficult jobs, such as the completely capsized battleships and *Shaw,* with its bow blasted off, were worked on next.

Early on it was decided not to pursue complete salvage of *Arizona*. Six days after the attack, the senior surviving officer from *Arizona* forwarded the ship's action report to Commander-in-Chief Pacific Fleet and noted, "The USS *Arizona* is a total loss except the

following is believed salvageable: fifty caliber machine guns in maintop, searchlights on after searchlight platform, the low catapult on quarterdeck and the guns of numbers 3 and 4 turrets." Removal of the ship's safes, personal belongings and valuables, and classified and sensitive documents was the first order of business in early 1942. Around this time, as many as 105 bodies were recovered. Salvage of the masts and super-structure followed. The toppled foremast was cut free on 5 May 1942, followed by the mainmast on 23 August. The stern aircraft crane and conning tower were removed in December 1942. Portions of the forecastle and the forward sections of the hull were cut free and raised, and holes were cut into the hull to remove equipment and give the salvage crews access to the wreck.

In early June 1942 the commandant of the navy yard recommended abandoning work on *Arizona* because it was a "task of great magnitude entailing the diversion of large men and equipment from other work." The ease of salvage was the deciding factor because time and expenses were mounting as the Navy raised the Pacific Fleet from the mud of Pearl Harbor. *Arizona*'s damage was such that the only way to completely salvage the ship would have been to build a cofferdam, but the harbor's coral bottom was too porous for a cofferdam to be effective. By December 1942 the decision not to raise or salvage *Arizona* had been made, and on the first of the month the battleship was stricken from the Navy Register.

Despite this decision, more of the ship was salvaged. With the exception of the No. 1 turret, which suffered extreme damage from the blast (its gun trunnions appear to have been sheared, and the gun barrels are depressed at an unnatural angle), all other ordnance and ammunition was removed in 1943. The 14-inch guns in Nos. 2, 3, and 4 turrets and all 5-inch/51-caliber secondary batteries were salvaged. The aft sections were partially dewatered, and ammunition was removed from the ships' magazines. The removal of the Nos. 3 and 4 turrets included the armored turrets themselves as well as the guns, their rotating parts, and the hoisting mechanisms.

To Lenihan and Murphy, this work appeared to fit a behavior described by anthropologist Richard Gould in his book *Shipwreck Anthropology*. Gould studied both the wrecks of the Spanish Armada of 1588 and airplane crashes from the Battle of Britain in 1940 and found that "the greater the defensive isolation of the combatants, the greater will be the efforts by that combatant to salvage and recycle items and/or materials of strategic value from any wrecks that fall within its territory." The salvage of the Nos. 3 and 4 turrets from *Arizona* are specific evidence of this sense of strategic vulnerability.

The turret mechanisms, armor, and guns were used to equip two coastal-defense batteries, one at Mokapu Head and the other up the slopes of the Wianae Mountains on Oahu's western shore. The installation at Mokapu, Battery Pennsylvania, was completed and test fired in mid-August 1945, four days before the Japanese surrender. After the war, both batteries were abandoned and the guns and machinery cut up for scrap. Nonetheless, these installations, regardless of their ultimate fate, were built and armed with *Arizona*'s guns in anticipation of a Japanese battleship assault, in which case battleship gun to battleship gun (the United States' being on land, of course) would slug it out. It was not an unusual concept. On the mainland near San Francisco, 16-inch guns destined for battleships never built were mounted in casemated concrete and earth batteries.

The archaeological work at Pearl Harbor was done in close partnership with the Navy's Mobile Diving and Salvage Unit One, headquartered at Pearl Harbor and then commanded by Commander David McCampbell, whose father was the top-ranking U.S. naval ace of World War II. With Captain J. K. "Otto" Orzech, McCampbell and Lenihan inaugurated a successful program known as "Project Seamark." Seamark exercises combined Navy and National Park Service teams to assess sunken ships and other submerged relics not only of World War II but also of other periods, mostly in the Pacific. Seamark has now grown into a nationwide program and has extended into the Pacific to look at other warships, including wrecks in Guam and Palau, at Kiska in the Aleutian Islands, and at Bikini Atoll, where lies the A-bombed fleet of Operation Crossroads, including Admiral Yamamoto's flagship, *Nagato,* on whose decks he paced while awaiting word of the Pearl Harbor attack.

Arizona Today

*A*rizona lies in thirty-eight feet of water off Ford
Island in Pearl Harbor. It is located at berth F-7, to
which it was moored on the morning of 7 December
1941, crossed athwartship by the modern memorial that
spans its hulk. Only a small number of bodies were
recovered; because several hundred members of the
ship's complement lie entombed inside the hulk, *Arizona*
was left as a war grave and later became a memorial.

Archaeological surveys of the submerged hulk of
Arizona in 1983, 1984, 1986, and 1987 determined that the
battleship lies at a five-to-ten degree list to port and,
while intact, readily evidences the severity of her battle
damage. The hull just aft of the bow is distorted and
cracked from gunwale to keel on the port side and
nearly so on the starboard side, indicating that the bow
was nearly blown off. The explosion also blew the
armored deck forward; torn and twisted portions of the
deck are folded together near the bow, with one large

section of deck peeled back toward the port bow and jutting over the side of the hull. Debris, mostly twisted and torn fragments of steel and numerous miscellaneous fittings, litters the decks. Surprisingly, even in this severely damaged area, the battleship's teak decks remain intact and undeteriorated except for areas where silt does not offer protection. A thick growth of barnacles, oysters, sponges, corals, grasses, and sea anemones covers the hull, retarding corrosion; nonetheless, the starboard side of the battleship shows more corrosion, with loose hull plates that flex and shift with current and tidal flow. Perhaps the most striking feature is the rows of deadlights, blast covers still fixed, that line the hull. Some have air trapped between blast cover and the glass of the deadlight and provide an eerie reminder that *Arizona* is the watery grave of some nine hundred men.

The first major feature aft of the bow is the No. 1 turret. With its three 14-inch guns trained forward in a slightly depressed elevation, this turret dropped intact with the deck when the latter collapsed. The guns and machinery, as well as the top of the No. 2 turret, have been removed, but the armored sides and back plate of the turret mark its position, with the tops of the turret sides visible just above the surface of the water at low tide. The bottom portion of the superstructure remains intact; its formerly enclosed spaces are discernible through the stubs of bulkheads and features such as the base of *Arizona*'s stack, the blue and white checked tiles of the galley, and the legs of galley stoves and other kitchen equipment, which remain attached to the deck. A surprising array of small artifacts litter this area; among them are dishes and silverware. It is at this spot that the *Arizona* Memorial spans the wreck, and the superstructure forms the basic outline of the ship that visitors see on one side of the Memorial.

Aft of the superstructure, the stub of the battleship's

mainmast rises toward the surface; welded to it is the steel flagstaff from which the memorial's flag flies.

Aft of the mainmast is the barbette for the No. 3 turret, which rises above the surface of the water. The round barbette is the most prominent above-water feature of the battleship. Attached on supports to the port side of the turret's barbette and on the port side of the former bridge area are the rusting remains of steel and concrete quays that were constructed in 1942 as a new battleship berth.

Aft of the No. 3 turret is the submerged barbette of the No. 4 turret. It is there, in this dark cavern, that Navy divers place the cremated remains of *Arizona*'s survivors who wish to be interned with their shipmates.

At the stern itself, the raised letters forming *Arizona*'s name are present. The socket for the jackstaff at the apex of the stern, now several feet beneath the surface, serves as yet another reminder of the ship's loss. It inevitably recalls Kleber Masterson and Leon Grabowsky's last trip to the ship to recover the stained and tattered ensign flying there on the evening of 7 December.

The arched, white concrete Arizona *Memorial spans the shattered, sunken hulk of the battleship.*

Bibliography

The artist consulted the following sources while researching his paintings:

Alden, John D., Commander, USN (Ret.). *Flush Decks and Four Pipes*. Annapolis: Naval Institute Press, 1989.

Army of the U.S., Document No. 91, June 7, 1939.

Baker, A. D., III, introduction. *Japanese Naval Vessels of World War II: As Seen by U.S. Naval Intelligence*. Annapolis: Naval Institute Press, 1987.

Barker, A. J. *Pearl Harbor*. New York: Ballantine Books, 1969.

Bell, Dana. *Air Force Colors*. vol. 1. Carrollton, Texas: Squadron/Signal Publications, Inc., 1926, 1942.

Caidin, Martin. *Zero Fighter*.

Carpenter, Dorr P. and Norman Polmar. *Submarines of the Imperial Japanese Navy*. Annapolis: Naval Institute Press, 1986.

Christy, Joe and Jeff Ethell. *P-40 Hawks at War*. Charles Scribner's Sons, 1980.

Collier's Photographic History of WWII.

Davis, Larry. *B-17 in Action*. Carrollton, Texas: Squadron/Signal Publications, Inc., 1984.

Francillon, Rene J. *Japanese Aircraft of the Pacific War*. New York: Funk & Wagnells, 1970.

————. *Japanese Navy Bombers of World War Two*. Garden City: Doubleday, 1971.

Freeman, Roger A. *B-17: Fortress at War*. London: 1977.

Friedman, Norman. *U.S. Battleships: An Illustrated Design History*. Annapolis: Naval Institute Press, 1985.

————. *U.S. Cruisers: An Illustrated Design History*. Annapolis: Naval Institute Press, 1984.

Friedman, Norman; Arthur D. Baker III; Arnold S. Lott, LCDR, USN (Ret.); and Robert F. Sumrall, HTC, USNR. *USS Arizona (BB39)*. Annapolis: Leeward Publications, 1978.

Hata, Ikuhiko and Yasuho Izawa. *Japanese Naval Aces and Fighter Units in World War II*. Translated by Don Cyril Gorham. Annapolis: Naval Institute Press, 1989.

Japanese Military Aircraft Illustrated, Koku-Fan. Volume 1, Fighters. Volume 2, Reconnaissance/Trainers/Transport. Volume 3, Bombers.

Jentschura, Hansgeorg, Dieter Jung, and Peter Michel. *Warships of the Imperial Japanese Navy, 1869-1945*. Translated by Antony Preston and J. D. Brown. Annapolis: Naval Institute Press, 1977.

Jones, Lloyd S. *U.S. Bombers, 1928 to 1980s*. Fallbrook, CA: Aero Publishers, 1984.

154

Katcher, Philip. *The U.S. Army 1941–1945*. London: Osprey Publishing Ltd., 1984.

Lawson, Robert L., ed. *The History of U.S. Naval Air Power*. New York: The Military Press, 1985.

Lenihan, Daniel J., ed. *Submerged Cultural Resources Study: USS Arizona Memorial and Pearl Harbor National Historic Landmark*. Southwest Cultural Resources Center, Professional Papers, No. 23. Santa Fe, New Mexico: National Park Service, 1989.

Lewis, Emanuel Raymond. *Seacoast Fortifications of the United States: An Introductory History*. Washington, D.C.: Smithsonian Institution Press, 1970.

Lott, Arnold S. and Robert F. Sumrall. *Pearl Harbor Attack*. Annapolis: Leeward Publications, 1977.

McDowell, Ernest. *Curtiss P-40 in Action*. Carrollton, Texas: Squadron/Signal Publications, Inc., 1976.

Mikesh, Robert C. *Zero Fighter*. New York: Crown Publishers, 1980.

Nohara, Shigeru. *A6M Zero in Action*. Carrollton, Texas: Squadron/Signal Publications, Inc., 1983.

Reilly, John C. *U.S. Navy Destroyers of WWII*. Dorset, Great Britain: 1983.

Roscoe, Theodore. *United States Destroyer Operations in World War II*. Annapolis: Naval Institute Press, 1953.

———. *United States Submarine Operations in World War II*. Annapolis: Naval Institute Press, 1949.

Scarborough, W. E., Captain, USN (Ret.). *PBY in Action*. Carrollton, TX: Squadron/Signal Publications, Inc., 1983.

Siefring, Thomas A. *U.S. Air Force in WWII*. London: Bison Books, 1982.

Silverstone, Paul H. *U.S. Warships of World War II*. Garden City: Doubleday, 1965.

Smith, Bob. *PBM Mariner in Action*. Carrollton, Texas: Squadron/Signal Publications, Inc.

Smith, Myron D., Jr. *Keystone Battlewagon, USS Pennsylvania (BB-38)*. Charleston, West Virginia: Pictorial Histories Publishing Company, 1983.

Sowinski, Larry. *Action in the Pacific: As Seen by U.S. Navy Photographers during World War 2*. Annapolis: Naval Institute Press, 1981.

Stern, Robert. *U.S. Navy 1942–1943*. London: Arms and Armor Press, 1990.

Stern, Robert C. *U.S. Battleships in Action*. Carrollton, Texas: Squadron/Signal Publications, Inc., 1980.

Stillwell, Paul, ed. *Air Raid: Pearl Harbor! Recollections of a Day of Infamy*. Annapolis: Naval Institute Press, 1981.

Terzibaschitsch, Stefan. *Aircraft Carriers of the U.S. Navy*. 2nd edition. Annapolis: Naval Institute Press, 1989.

U.S. Navy Carrier Bombers of WWII. Carrollton, Texas: Squadron/Signal Publications, Inc., 1987.

U.S. Navy Carrier Fighters of WWII. Carrollton, Texas: Squadron/Signal Publications, Inc., 1987.

Ward, Richard. *Curtiss P-40D-N Warhawk in USAAF*. New York: Arco Publishing Co., 1969.

Watts, Anthony John. *Japanese Warships of World War II*. Garden City: Doubleday, 1967.

In writing the commentary, the author consulted the following sources:

Brown, DeSoto. *Hawaii Goes to War*. Honolulu: Editions Unlimited, 1989.

Cohen, Stan. *East Wind Rain: A Pictorial History of the Pearl Harbor Attack*. Missoula, Montana: Pictorial Histories, 1981.

Conroy, Hilary, and Harry Wray. *Pearl Harbor Reexamined: Prologue to the Pacific War*. Honolulu: University of Hawaii Press, 1990.

Cressman, Robert J., and J. Michael Wenger. *Steady Nerves and Stout Hearts: The Enterprise (CV6) Air Group and Pearl Harbor, 7 December 1941*. Missoula, Montana: Pictorial Histories, 1989.

Ewing, Steve. *Memories and Memorials: The World War II US Navy 40 Years After Victory*. Missoula, Montana: Pictorial Histories Pub. Co., 1986.

Friedman, Norman; Arthur D. Baker III; Arnold S. Lott, LCDR, USN (Ret.); and Robert F. Sumrall, HTC, USNR. *USS Arizona (BB39)*. Annapolis: Leeward Publications, 1978.

Gould, Richard A., ed. *Shipwreck Anthropology*. Albuquerque: University of New Mexico Press, 1983.

———. *Recovering the Past*. Albuquerque: University of New Mexico Press, 1990.

Lenihan, Daniel J., ed. *Submerged Cultural Resources Study: USS Arizona Memorial and Pearl Harbor National Historic Landmark*. Southwest Cultural Resources Center, Professional Papers, No. 23. Santa Fe, New Mexico: National Park Service, 1989.

Lord, Walter. *Day of Infamy*. New York: Holt, Rinehart & Co., 1957.

Lott, Arnold S., and Robert F. Sumrall. *USS Ward-The First*

Shot. St. Paul, Minnesota: The First Shot Naval Vets, 1983.

Murphy, Joy Waldron. "Diving Into the Past: A Rare View of Pearl Harbor." *Impact/Albuquerque Journal Magazine* (March 10, 1987).

Prange, Gordon W., Donald M. Goldstein, and Katherine V. Dillon. *At Dawn We Slept: The Untold Story of Pearl Harbor.* New York: McGraw-Hill, 1981.

———. *Pearl Harbor: The Verdict of History.* New York: McGraw-Hill, 1986.

———. *December 7, 1941: The Day the Japanese Attacked Pearl Harbor.* New York: McGraw-Hill, 1988.

———. *God's Samurai: Lead Pilot at Pearl Harbor.* Washington and New York: Brassey's (US), Inc., 1990.

Ross, Donald K., and Helen L. Ross. *0755: The Heroes of Pearl Harbor.* Port Orchard, Washington: Rokalu Press, 1988.

Sakamaki, Kazuo. *I Attacked Pearl Harbor.* New York: Association Press, 1949.

Sheehan, Ed. *Days of '41: Pearl Harbor Remembered.* Honolulu: Pearl Harbor-Honolulu Branch 46, Fleet Reserve Association Enterprises, 1976.

Slackman, Michael. *Remembering Pearl Harbor: The Story of the USS Arizona Memorial.* Honolulu: *Arizona* Memorial Museum Association, 1984.

———, ed. *Pearl Harbor in Perspective.* Honolulu: *Arizona* Memorial Museum Association, 1986.

———. *Target: Pearl Harbor.* Honolulu: University of Hawaii Press and the *Arizona* Memorial Museum Association, 1990.

Smith, Myron D., Jr. *Keystone Battlewagon, USS Pennsylvania (BB-38).* Charleston, West Virginia: Pictorial Histories Publishing Company, 1983.

Stillwell, Paul, ed. *Air Raid: Pearl Harbor! Recollections of a Day of Infamy.* Annapolis: Naval Institute Press, 1981.

Wallin, Vice Admiral Homer N., USN (Ret.). *Pearl Harbor: Why, How, Fleet Salvage and Final Appraisal.* Washington, D.C.: Naval History Division, 1968.

Young, Stephen Bower. "Out of the Darkness." U.S. Naval Institute *Proceedings* (December 1965).

Index

159

About the Artist

Drama and action are the hallmarks of a Freeman product. While he paints an occasional portrait of a ship, the thirty-eight-year-old artist wants to depict action, be it a sixty-foot wave rolling with majestic violence into the bow of a ship or the bright red tracery of shells arcing across the night sky.

Born in Pontiac, Michigan, near Detroit, Freeman watched ships pass without pause on the busy St. Claire River linking Lakes Huron and Erie. Early in his life he was well aware of the harsh reality of life at sea, for his father took him to see a capsized wreck rising out of the muddy St. Claire. "I had never seen anything like that ship. It made a powerful impression on me." Ever since, Freeman's paintings of choice have made a powerful impression on others. "I want people to look at my painting and see it, smell it, and feel it. I want my work to arouse all the senses."

Working from his memory of experiences before the mast in the North Atlantic, and in the Marine Corps and Army, Tom Freeman has created an impressive portfolio. His works have appeared on the covers of various books and magazines, including the U.S. Naval Institute *Proceedings*, as well as inside many publications, as poster art and limited-edition lithographs, on Maryland's first Saltwater Sport Fishing Stamp, and on limited-edition porcelain plates produced by the Franklin Mint and the Hamilton Plate Group. Recently, Freeman produced three large murals for the United States Naval Academy, depicting a large carrier task force at sea, a submarine rescuing a downed B-52's crew, and the Battle of Hue.

Sponsors of Freeman's work include corporations such as Martin Marietta, publishing houses, and the National Park Service. His works hang in several national park visitor centers, and his paintings have been hung in numerous galleries and in the West Wing of the White House.

About the Author

James P. Delgado takes a hands-on approach to history. The thirty-three-year-old historian and underwater archaeologist spent thirteen years with the National Park Service (NPS), working not only in archives but also on the ocean floor. Musty photographs, dusty logbooks, and dim memories take firm shape as Delgado investigates sunken ships. As a member of the federal government's only working team of underwater archaeologists, the NPS's Submerged Cultural Resources Unit, Delgado participated in an underwater survey of Pearl Harbor that included the mapping and study of the hulks of *Arizona* and *Utah*.

His work also took him to the distant reaches of Bikini Atoll, two thousand miles west of Hawaii, where he dived on the wrecks of several vessels, including Yamamoto's flagship *Nagato* and the carrier *Saratoga*, both victims of Operation Crossroads, the United States' 1946 tests of the atomic bomb. He recently led an expedition to Veracruz, Mexico, where he and other American archaeologists represented the United States in a joint exploration of the wreck of the U.S. brig *Somers*, lost in 1846. A near mutiny on *Somers* in 1842 resulted in three executions and inspired Herman Melville's novella *Billy Budd*.

As the Maritime Historian of the NPS, Delgado conducted the studies that resulted in *Arizona*'s and *Utah*'s designation as National Historic Landmarks. His studies of the yard tug *Hoga* (YT-146) and the midget submarine *HA-19*, captured as a prize of war on 8 December, spurred the designation of these vessels as national landmarks also.

Delgado has authored eleven books and several dozen articles, which have been published in *California History*, *The American Neptune*, the U.S. Naval Institute *Proceedings*, *Naval History*, and other magazines. His work has focused on the naval and maritime history of the mid-19th century and World War II. His most recent book, *To California By Sea: A Maritime History of the Gold Rush* (University of South Carolina Press, 1990), met with considerable public and scholarly acclaim. In addition to preparing the text for *Pearl Harbor Recalled*, he has recently completed *Ghosts of the Atomic Age: The Sunken Ships of Bikini Atoll* and, with J. Candace Clifford, *Great American Ships*, a guide to every historic vessel accessible to the public in the United States.

Named executive director of the Vancouver Maritime Museum in 1991, Delgado and his family now reside in British Columbia.

The **Naval Institute Press** is the book-publishing arm of the U.S. Naval Institute, a private, nonprofit professional society for members of the sea services and civilians who share an interest in naval and maritime affairs. Established in 1873 at the U.S. Naval Academy in Annapolis, Maryland, where its offices remain today, the Naval Institute has more than 100,000 members worldwide.

Members of the Naval Institute receive the influential monthly magazine *Proceedings* and discounts on fine nautical prints, ship and aircraft photos, and subscriptions to the quarterly *Naval History* magazine. They also have access to the transcripts of the Institute's Oral History Program and get discounted admission to any of the Institute-sponsored seminars offered around the country.

The Naval Institute's book-publishing program, begun in 1898 with basic guides to naval practices, has broadened its scope in recent years to include books of more general interest. Now the Naval Institute Press publishes more than sixty titles each year, ranging from how-to books on boating and navigation to battle histories, biographies, ship and aircraft guides, and novels. Institute members receive discounts on the Press's nearly 400 books in print.

Full-time students are eligible for special half-price membership rates. Life memberships are also available.

For a free catalog describing the Naval Institute Press books currently available, and for further information about U.S. Naval Institute membership, please write to:

Membership & Communications Department
U.S. Naval Institute
118 Maryland Avenue
Annapolis, Maryland 21402-5035

Or call, toll-free, (800) 233-8764.

THE NAVAL INTITUTE PRESS

PEARL HARBOR RECALLED

New Images of the Day of Infamy

Designed by Pamela Lewis Schnitter

Set in Palatino and Caslon 224 Black
in Adobe Post Script on a Macintosh IIci
and output by York Graphics, York,
Pennsylvania

Printed on 80-lb Warren Cameo Dull
and bound in Kingston Natural with Papan
Homespun endsheets by Strine Printing
Company, York, Pennsylvania